learning that sticks

Other ASCD/McREL copublications:

The 12 Touchstones of Good Teaching: A Checklist
for Staying Focused Every Day
by Bryan Goodwin and Elizabeth Ross Hubbell

Balanced Leadership for Powerful Learning:
Tools for Achieving Success in Your School
by Bryan Goodwin and Greg Cameron with Heather Hein

Classroom Instruction That Works (2nd Edition)
by Ceri B. Dean, Elizabeth Ross Hubbell, Howard Pitler, and Bj Stone

Classroom Instruction That Works
with English Language Learners (2nd Edition)
by Jane Hill and Kirsten Miller

A Handbook for Classroom Instruction That Works
by Howard Pitler and Bj Stone

School Leadership That Works: From Research to Results
by Robert J. Marzano, Timothy Waters, and Brian A. McNulty

Simply Better: Doing What Matters Most
to Change the Odds for Student Success
by Bryan Goodwin

Understanding Common Core State Standards
by John Kendall

Unstuck: How Curiosity, Peer Coaching, and Teaming Can Change Your School
by Bryan Goodwin, Kristin Rouleau, Dale Lewis, and Tonia Gibson

Using Technology with Classroom Instruction That Works
by Elizabeth Ross Hubbell, Howard Pitler, and Matt Kuhn

learning that sticks

A Brain-Based Model for K–12 Instructional Design and Delivery

BRYAN GOODWIN

with TONIA GIBSON and KRISTIN ROULEAU

ASCD

Alexandria, Virginia USA

McREL
INTERNATIONAL

Denver, Colorado USA

1703 N. Beauregard St. • Alexandria, VA 22311-1714 USA
Phone: 800-933-2723 or 703-578-9600 • Fax: 703-575-5400
Website: www.ascd.org • E-mail: member@ascd.org
Author guidelines: www.ascd.org/write

McREL International
4601 DTC Boulevard, Suite 500
Denver, CO 80237 USA
Phone: 303-337-0990 • Fax: 303-337-3005
Website: www.mcrel.org • E-mail: info@mcrel.org

Ranjit Sidhu, *CEO and Executive Director;* Stefani Roth, *Publisher;* Genny Ostertag, *Director, Content Acquisitions;* Julie Houtz, *Director, Book Editing & Production;* Jamie Greene, *Editor;* Judi Connelly, *Senior Art Director;* Georgia Park, *Senior Graphic Designer;* Kelly Marshall, *Manager, Production Services;* Valerie Younkin, *Senior Production Designer;* Trinay Blake, *E-Publishing Specialist*

PAPERBACK ISBN: 978-1-4166-2910-8   ASCD product #120032   n06/20
PDF E-BOOK ISBN: 978-1-4166-2912-2; see Books in Print for other formats.
Quantity discounts are available: e-mail programteam@ascd.org or call 800-933-2723, ext. 5773, or 703-575-5773.
For desk copies, go to www.ascd.org/deskcopy.

Library of Congress Cataloging-in-Publication Data
Names: Goodwin, Bryan, author. | Gibson, Tonia, author. | Rouleau, Kristin, author. | Mid-continent Research for Education and Learning (Organization), issuing body.
Title: Learning that sticks : a brain-based model for K-12 instructional design and delivery / Bryan Goodwin with Tonia Gibson, Kristin Rouleau.
Description: Alexandria, VA : ASCD ; Denver, CO : McREL, [2020] | Includes bibliographical references and index. | Summary: "This book helps teachers learn the basics of how the brain-and-learning-works so they can focus less on TEACHING and get LEARNING to "stick""—Provided by publisher.
Identifiers: LCCN 2020007086 (print) | LCCN 2020007087 (ebook) | ISBN 9781416629108 (paperback) | ISBN 9781416629122 (pdf)
Subjects: LCSH: Learning, Psychology of. | Cognitive learning. | Teaching—Psychological aspects. | Instructional systems—Design.
Classification: LCC LB1060 .G664 2020 (print) | LCC LB1060 (ebook) | DDC 370.15/23—dc23
LC record available at https://lccn.loc.gov/2020007086
LC ebook record available at https://lccn.loc.gov/2020007087

27 26 25 24 23 22 21 20   1 2 3 4 5 6 7 8 9 10 11 12

A Brain-Based Model
for K–12 Instructional Design and Delivery

Check out this related ASCD/McREL copublication:

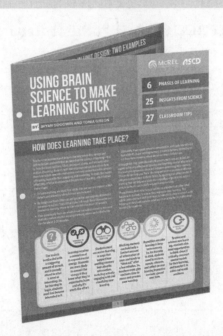

Using Brain Science to Make Learning Stick (Quick Reference Guide)
by Bryan Goodwin & Tonia Gibson (#QRG120087)

Preface: Why a Learning Model?

If somebody offered you a thousand dollars to draw a reasonably accurate model of the human circulatory system, you'd probably be a thousand dollars richer a few minutes later—even if you're not a doctor. You know there's the heart, veins carrying unoxygenated blood back to the heart, and arteries carrying oxygenated blood to the muscles and organs of the body. Since oxygen is involved, you know the lungs must figure into it somehow. Given a few minutes of thinking, you'd likely to be able to sketch out a workable model, including labeling some of the key parts, and in the process use modestly technical vocabulary.

Basically, you can sort out how we breathe in oxygen and distribute it to our body's cells and expel depleted carbon dioxide from our bodies. That's because circulation ceased being a mystery several centuries ago, so we all learned about it in school. Even though it's something we can't observe with our own eyes (on a good day, anyway), all of us know the basics of it.

If you're reading this book, however, odds are you're a teacher rather than a cardiologist, so try this: See if you can draw a model of the human learning system—that is, how information enters our brains and gets converted into long-term memories we can retrieve later. In other words, how do our brains "breathe in" information to store and retrieve for later use? What's the process? What are the key vocabulary terms?

I'll give you some time.

It's a bit of a stumper, isn't it? Don't feel bad if you struggled with this thought experiment. I've tried it with hundreds of teachers, principals, and administrators from across the United States and around the world over the last few years and found it's a challenge for nearly everyone.

Nevertheless, there *is* a human learning system. Although its parts and processes may have remained concealed from science somewhat longer than blood vessels were, cognitive scientists have known for decades (a century or more when it comes to certain aspects) much about how the brain processes information into long-term memory. Therefore, this knowledge is something we should know, especially if we're educators.

Think about it this way. Would you agree to undergo brain surgery from a doctor who did not know the anatomy of the brain or what impact various surgical techniques would have on it? Well, teaching is like performing noninvasive brain surgery on a classroom full of patients, 180 days a year. To do that well, we need to know a thing or two about how the brain works and be able to translate that understanding into designing learning experiences for students.

Learning How to Make Learning Stick

Many teachers, through no fault of their own, often know little about how learning actually works. Somehow, even though cognitive science—what we might call the science of learning—has been around for decades, it's not adequately covered in many teacher preparation programs. In fact, a study of dozens of popular textbooks in preservice programs found that *none* of them accurately describe six key instructional strategies grounded in the science of learning (Greenberg, Pomerance & Walsh, 2016). As a result, according to the reports' authors, new teachers are not learning "the most fundamental information needed to make learning 'stick'" (p. v). They often enter classrooms with an incomplete toolkit, which can leave them frustrated and overwhelmed and leave students shortchanged.

This book aims to correct that by providing you with these research-based teaching strategies (and others) so you can deliver better learning for students. Instead of just spoon-feeding them to you, this book will unpack the cognitive science underlying these strategies so you can sequence them into learning experiences that challenge, inspire, and engage your students. As a result, you'll learn to teach with more intentionality—understanding not just *what* to do but also *when* and *why* to do it. You'll also know what to do when things go wrong or your students struggle to master new learning.

Looking into the "Black Box" of Students' Minds

Now it's time for true confessions. I knew very little of this stuff when I first entered the classroom. Sure, I had some best practices up my sleeve—asking higher-order questions, modeling processes for students, providing feedback, and the like. Admittedly, though, I knew little about *why* such things were best practices—that is, *how* they supported student learning. Back then, I had little idea what was happening inside students' minds while I was teaching. I just figured I needed to teach them something, have them practice it, test them on it, and hope it stuck.

If you'd visited my classroom in those days, you likely would've seen me doing many of the "right things."

Asking thought-provoking questions? Check!

Forming cooperative groups? Check!

Providing feedback? Check! And with a *green* pen to be nice. Double check!

Yet if you'd asked me *why* I was doing any of those things, such as putting kids in cooperative groups, I likely would have offered a blank stare. Maybe, on a good day, I might have said something like, "Well, I've been doing a lot of talking at the kids this week, so I figured they needed a break from that."

That wouldn't have been much of an answer, of course, yet it's not a whole lot different from what I—and my colleagues, including Kris and Tonia—have heard some educators say when we ask them why they're using certain practices in their classrooms. In many ways, it was hearing these things in so many places and so often that led me down the winding path to writing this book.

Why This Book

My colleagues' and my journey began several years ago, when ASCD and McREL published two editions of *Classroom Instruction That Works* (Dean, Hubbell, Pitler, & Stone, 2012; Marzano, Pickering, & Pollock, 2001), which remains one of the most popular books on instruction ever printed. In these books, we identified several "high-leverage" teaching strategies. Following their publication, we spent countless hours in schools and classrooms helping teachers use the strategies. While visiting classrooms and watching educators in action, something began to trouble us.

At first, we thought perhaps we were just seeing some earnest yet novice attempts to apply best practices. Some teachers, for example, seemed to think that if *a little bit* of cooperative learning was good, then a *whole bunch of it* ought to be even better—to the point that we'd see students in their classrooms sitting in small groups reading textbooks together ("to ask each other questions if they get stuck"), which hardly reflected effective cooperative learning. Yet their teachers seemed to think they were doing the right things—after all, research says cooperative learning works!

Meanwhile, we bumped into more than a few principals who were dogged in their pursuit of doing what works—to the point that they would hammer on teachers to use, say, similarities and differences ad nauseum regardless of whether teachers knew when or why to engage students in the mental exercise of comparing and contrasting. On one level, they were engaging in the "right" things, yet their reasons for doing so were often shallow or misguided.

It wasn't all bad, though. We saw a lot of good things happening, too, especially when teachers and entire school teams became increasingly intentional with evidence-based teaching practices—that is, thinking about *why* they were using them. When that happened, student engagement and learning increased significantly.

In a subsequent ASCD/McREL book on teaching, *The 12 Touchstones of Good Teaching* (Goodwin & Hubbell, 2013), we highlighted the need for teachers to provide challenging, engaging, and *intentional* instruction and showed how the strategies in *Classroom Instruction That Works* supported student learning (i.e., pairing the *what* with the *why*). We hoped that revealing the *why* behind the *what* would help teachers connect the dots and select the appropriate teaching strategy for the learning task at hand.

However, we still found teachers often approached lesson planning solely in terms of their own moves and not what they wanted students to be doing or thinking about. They might follow a lesson plan template but not really consider what ought to happen in students' minds at each step along the way. As a result, lessons were often a string of activities that didn't engage or challenge students. In short, the focus was often on teaching, not learning.

Teaching with Learning in Mind

That's when we knew something was missing for many teachers—namely, a deep understanding of what should be going on in students' minds when they were engaging in learning activities. After all, that's where the real "action" occurs in any classroom. For many teachers, though (ourselves included, before we dug more deeply into the science of learning), students' minds have largely been something of a black box. As a result, when learning breaks down, we're not really sure what went wrong or what to do differently to help students learn.

It doesn't have to be that way.

This book will help you to peer inside that black box. It covers the basics of how the brain reacts to new information, how it stores memories away for later use, and how it retrieves memories and applies prior learning to new situations. Along the way, you may find you need to unlearn some of what you thought you knew about learning. As we'll see, what scientists have discovered over the years about learning often runs counter to some "tried and true" learning strategies most of us have used because we think they work—yet only have the illusion of working.

Filling the Gap Between Research on Instruction and the Science of Learning

In important ways, this book is unlike any others on your shelf or in your e-book reader.

Yes, you can find plenty of books that tell you what (hopefully research-based) instructional strategies to employ, but rarely do they ground their recommendations in the science of learning. As a result, they may help you solve a particular problem of practice but do little to help you consider what ought to be going on in your students' minds to engage them in deep learning. You're unlikely to develop insights into why a particular strategy works, when you ought to use it, and when it might no longer work.

At the other end of the spectrum, you can find a burgeoning collection of books that provide insights on the science of learning and brain science. Such books have their place, too, especially for expert practitioners who are ready to dig into neuroscience—a fascinating field that's beginning to bear some fruit for educators. Yet it's often a long walk back from neuropeptides to the realities of teaching a couple dozen youngsters in a classroom. As a result, brain science can be a bit overwhelming for teachers who have a lesson plan to prepare, papers to grade, and a faculty meeting at 3:30 p.m.

This book is designed with that reality in mind—that you have a lesson or unit plan to get ready by tomorrow. It's not going to provide a postdoctorate-level deep dive into the brain's electrochemistry, synapses, and dendrites. Instead, it will summarize the big ideas that have emerged from cognitive psychology—the study of learning—over the past few decades and their implications for teaching and learning in your classroom.

On one level, this book will help you "zoom out" to get a better grasp of the process of learning from beginning to end. On a deeper level, it will also help you "zoom in" to see what's going on in students' minds during each phase of the process, including what "blockages" or "leaks" may occur as students engage in learning so you can adjust your teaching strategies accordingly. In so doing, this book will demystify the process of learning and hopefully provide you with a number of a-ha moments about students' learning along the way, helping you to set aside counterproductive practices that can get in the way of learning and ultimately making learning more productive and joyful in your classroom.

Providing a Model for Learning

What is perhaps most unique about this book is it offers a model for learning that draws from the most salient ideas from the science of learning you can apply in your classroom. As it turns out, providing such a model reflects a key insight from the science of learning itself—that we learn best when we "extract the key ideas from new material and organize them into a mental model" (Brown, Roediger, & McDaniel, 2014, p. 6). As you'll see later in this book, to retain information, we must make sense of it, connecting dots and grouping ideas together. One of the best ways to do this is to develop a mental representation of the world around us—one that's simple enough to allow us to zoom out and see how the parts fit together while being accurate and sophisticated enough to let us zoom in on key details.

Although researchers are still grappling with some of the finer details about how exactly the mind works, the processes described in this book reflect what cognitive scientists generally agree are the fundamental processes involved in translating information from our five senses into deep, long-term memories. Better teaching—teaching that supports deep learning—reflects the natural progression of knowledge through the stages of learning, which are shared in this book.

In summary, this book takes what we know from cognitive psychology, particularly what's called the information processing model, and translates it into a model for classroom lesson and unit design. Having a solid, workable mental model of learning will help you plan better learning opportunities for your students, diagnose and solve their learning challenges, and adjust your instruction accordingly—much as doctors use proven models of the circulatory system to diagnose and solve cardiovascular diseases.

Not Another Framework—A Model

At this point, you might be thinking, "Wait, I think my school or district already has a districtwide instructional model. Is this the same thing?"

Most likely not.

That's because what people often call instructional models aren't models at all; at best, they're frameworks of teaching practice. Yes, this may sound like splitting hairs, so let's take a moment to parse the difference between these two terms that often get bandied about interchangeably but have decidedly different meanings.

Models explain abstract phenomena and provide mental representations of how things work by describing a process, cycle, or sequence. For example, the water cycle provides meteorologists with a shared understanding of how water evaporates from the ocean, condenses into clouds, and returns to Earth as precipitation. In film and theater, playwrights and screenwriters often follow a three-act model to sequence scenes into narratives with rising action, conflict, and resolution. Essentially, models help us to make sense of procedural (how-to) knowledge by showing how things work and fit together sequentially. In other words, they show how to do something and often provide basic templates to emulate.

By contrast, frameworks arrange and structure declarative (factual) knowledge into categories, taxonomies, or mental "buckets." In literature, for example, we use frameworks to distinguish various genres of fiction (e.g., mystery, action, romance). In biology, we use a taxonomy first developed by Aristotle to categorize different types of living organisms (e.g., plants, mammals, reptiles, fish). With this in mind, most teacher evaluation systems and many so-called instructional models are actually frameworks—they categorize the myriad things we want teachers to attend to in their classrooms and professional lives (e.g., planning lessons, creating positive classroom climates, delivering instruction, engaging in collegial learning). In short, they clarify what to do yet not necessarily how to do it.

The *how* is where a model comes in.

As you dig into the model of learning described in this book, some astute readers may notice it has echoes of some popular instructional design models, such as Madeline Hunter, explicit direct instruction, and Robert Gagné's nine events of instruction (to name but a few). This is, in fact, true. This model has many similarities to these older models (which are also similar to one another). That's because most of them have shared roots in Benjamin Bloom's efforts in the 1960s and 1970s to develop a model of mastery learning based on cognitive science.

You'll notice, however, that unlike many of these earlier models, the Learning That Sticks model is not framed around steps teachers take to guide instruction (e.g., launch a lesson, check for understanding, create practice opportunities) but, rather, steps students take to engage in deep learning. In so doing, this book aims to stretch your thinking, "flipping" it to consider what ought to happen in students' minds as you're teaching so you can map your instructional moves onto what you can do to guide and support learning. In short, what's most important isn't what you are teaching but what students are learning.

How This Book Is Designed

This book is based on the simple premise that learning may be complicated, but learning about learning doesn't have to be. It takes big ideas from the science of learning and turns them into an easy-to-follow six-phase model of learning. Chapters 2–7 are named for what we've identified as the phases of learning, a progression we think you'll find logical, easy to grasp, and eminently applicable to your classroom, regardless of subject or grade level.

Each chapter helps you zoom out to the big picture of learning from beginning to end as well as zoom in on the details and practical implications, including teaching strategies that support each phase of learning. As a result, you'll be able to understand not only what to do but also when and why to use certain strategies.

After reading this book, you should be able to sketch out or explain a basic diagram of how the brain's cognitive system functions and the various stages of memory formation. If that sounds a bit cerebral or theoretical, don't worry. This book will also help you apply these insights to guide lesson and unit design in your classrooms along with plenty of practical tips you can use right away. At each step along the way, you'll get a toolkit of research-based teaching strategies you can use to support each phase of the learning process. All the while, you'll be able a draw a line of sight back to cognitive science to understand why a particular strategy is effective during a particular stage of learning.

A Starting Point, Not a Final Destination

Finally, keep in mind that this book isn't intended to offer a lock-step checklist for teachers. In practice, you'll likely find these phases of learning are not always linear; the process of learning in real life is often messier and more iterative. In short, this learning model is not intended to be a hard-and-fast script to follow but rather a springboard to more intentional and creative teaching.

Indeed, focusing on the science of learning is meant to encourage you to engage in deeper, more reflective professional practice as a teacher.

The point of this book is to help you design learning based on how your students' brains work, so you provide them with learning experiences that are not only challenging but also engaging and joyful. By the way, there's a word for this kind of engagement and joyful learning: *curiosity*. As you'll see, curiosity is an important driver of deep learning. When it's present, learning flourishes; when it's absent, learning withers. Now that you are hopefully feeling curious about student learning, let's dive into what's long been a black box for educators but doesn't need to be: our students' minds.

1

Understanding the Science of Learning

What you'll learn in this book isn't new or faddish. It's based on carefully designed studies of learning reported in peer-reviewed publications that have been around for many decades. Some of it, in fact, dates back to the 1870s when an amateur scientist in Germany, Hermann Ebbinghaus, began a series of unusual experiments on a singular subject—himself.

Each evening, at the same hour, Ebbinghaus would sit alone in a quiet room and pull from a box small sheets of paper with different nonsense syllables on each—drawn from a list of 2,300 nonsense syllables he carefully created (e.g., *mox, fim, tib*). After writing down each syllable in a notebook, he'd start a metronome and, following its rhythm, recite each syllable on the list in a monotone voice in equally spaced intervals. Afterward, he'd close his notebook and attempt to recall the list from memory, over and over, until he could recall them all.

From this lonely and tedious work, Ebbinghaus arrived at many important insights into the inner workings of our minds, including our "forgetting curve" (how quickly we forget new learning) and ways to strengthen memory (Boring, 1957). Perhaps most important, through his exacting and methodical experimentation, he began to turn what had previously been mostly just philosophical musings about the mind into a scientific pursuit, paving the way for study and exploration of how we learn.

The Information Processing Model

Starting in the 1950s, cognitive scientists developed what's commonly referred to as the *information processing model*, which uses the computer as an admittedly imperfect metaphor for what happens to information once it enters the brain. Basically, the information processing model attempts to map the long, perilous journey—full of twists, turns, and dead ends—that all new information must take before finding a home in our long-term memories. As you'll discover, the human brain is both shockingly powerful and maddeningly inconsistent. Sometimes it forgets things that its owner wishes desperately to remember (What's the name of my boss's husband? Where did I park the getaway car?). Sometimes it remembers things that its owner wishes desperately to forget (an unkind word or an annoying jingle).

In many ways, the challenge of learning is rooted in a fundamental paradox of the human brain. Although it can learn and retain staggering amounts of information, it's also incredibly adept at ignoring and forgetting information, which in many ways is a good thing. If we paid attention to every stimulus in our environment, we'd be nervous wrecks with our heads on a swivel, trying to pay attention to everything that's happening around us. And if we couldn't forget anything, we'd grow progressively unable to cope with the world as our brains clogged with useless information.

In fact, too much memory can be annoying—even lethal. Consider the curious case of Jill Price, who at first blush appears to possess what seems like a superpower: the ability to never forget. Now in her early 50s, she can recall events from her teens like they occurred yesterday. Ask her what she was doing on August 29, 1980, and she'll tell you, "It was a Friday. I went to Palm Springs with my friends, twins Nina and Michelle, and their family for Labor Day weekend."

The first time she heard Rick Springfield's "Jessie's Girl"? March 7, 1981. She was driving in a car with her mother yelling at her. The third time she drove a car? January 10, 1981. It was a Saturday. She was at "Teen Auto. That's where we used to get our driving lessons from" (McRobbie, 2017).

Price is among a group of rare people who have been clinically tested and found to have *hyperthymesia* or HSAM (highly superior autobiographical memory): the ability to recall abnormally vast details from their lives. They can remember minutiae from years earlier, such as every meal they've eaten, every phone number they've written down, and every song they've heard on the radio. Sounds awesome, yes? But in reality, not so much. Price will tell you that having "total recall" memory creates a swirling mess in her head and leaves her teetering on the edge of sanity.

> My memory has ruled my life. Whenever I see a date flash on the television (or anywhere else for that matter), I automatically go back to that day and remember where I was, what I was doing, what day it fell on,

and on and on and on and on. It is nonstop, uncontrollable and totally exhausting. . . . Most have called it a gift, but I call it a burden. I run my entire life through my head every day and it drives me crazy! (Parker, Cahill, & McGaugh, 2006, p. 35)

The Stages of Memory

Recent studies in neuroscience are finding that our brains appear actively and purposefully to forget most of what we learn—continually pruning and clearing out old and unneeded memories (often as we sleep) to allow us to focus on more important information. As it turns out, forgetting is as important to our memory systems as remembering (Richards & Frankland, 2017). Forgetting extraneous information simplifies our memories, decreasing the static hiss of the noisy, information-rich worlds in which we live and allowing us to focus on the pertinent details needed to make better decisions.

So, for the sake of our mental health and happiness, it's good that most of us ignore and forget the vast majority of what we experience. For learning, though? Not so great. As educators, we are locked in a constant battle with our students' brains, which by design are programmed to ignore or forget most of what's in their environment, including what we attempt to share with them in our classrooms. Therefore, let's take a look at the stages of memory, followed by the phases of learning with which they intersect, to build a mental model of the learning system.

Sensory Register: Finding a Signal in the Noise

Before memories can be created, we must notice some initial information with one or more of our five senses—sight, hearing, touch, taste, smell—or our related senses of movement and balance. Our nerves convert these stimuli into electrical signals that travel along our body's nerve fibers in milliseconds, racing with incredible urgency to arrive in our brains where—*surprise!*—the vast majority of stimuli are promptly discarded in less than a second.

Why does this happen? Well, there's simply too much going on around us every second of the day for our minds to remember it all in full detail. Our bodies are designed for survival in a hostile environment, and to survive, our early ancestors primarily needed to pay attention to and remember the really important stuff—things that kept us safe from predators, nourished, and sheltered. For example, it was important to be able to ignore our hunting companion prattling on about his digestive issues and narrow our focus down to a tiny pinhole of stimuli: a lion making its way toward us through the savannah grass while licking its chops. The ability to filter distractions down to a pinhole was a good thing—it was the difference between living to tell the tale and being a lion's lunch.

Even now, hundreds of thousands of years later, most of what we sense throughout our day can be simply ignored. In fact, our brains' ability to filter out distractions (which I'm doing right now as I write this paragraph on my laptop while sitting outdoors at my daughters' swim meet, surrounded by screaming kids, loud music, towels flapping in the breeze, and people walking by, to name but a few stimuli) is often essential in helping us focus on the stimuli that are most important to us at the moment. Yet as teachers, it means we must ensure students focus their "pinholes" on what we want them to learn.

The next time you walk into your school or office, try to observe and remember everything you're seeing, hearing, and feeling for as long as you can: the color and shape of every car in the parking lot, the conversations of people you pass by, the feeling of a light breeze or sun on your face, the clothes and facial expressions worn by every person you see. This is the sensory register, and it's impossible to hold on to every single input all at once and for any length of time. Only a tiny fraction of what registers gets retained. And as we'll see, "rules" in our brains form something of a pecking order for which information we pay attention to and which we ignore.

Stimuli that make it through the filters of our sensory registers and are deemed important enough can begin moving along a journey through three phases of memory: immediate, working, and long-term. This is true regardless of the type of memory in play, declarative or procedural, although the area of the brain that leaps into action varies. Declarative memory, which is the recall of facts, information, and personal experiences, is stored across the neocortex—the large, gray, wrinkly outer part of the brain—and deeper down, inside the hippocampus and the amygdala near the center of your brain. It is further divided into episodic memory (recollections of events we personally experience) and semantic memory (facts and information we have learned).

Procedural memory refers to the memories that allow us to repeat physical actions and skills, such as how to ride a bicycle or draw a portrait. These performance-based memories are stored in the basal ganglia and cerebellum, which coordinate our movement, balance, and equilibrium (Queensland Brain

Institute, n.d.). Experiments by neuroscientists have found that our procedural memories, once established, are very strong and far less likely to fade over time than our declarative memories, which is why we can remember how to ride a bicycle years after our last pedal around the block (Suchan, 2018).

Immediate Memory: The First 30 Seconds

Those lucky few sensory inputs that make it through our initial filters are carried along by electrical signals to neurons that then produce a biochemical charge that records, or encodes, the impression of that stimulus. Then it passes along this code to a thousand other neurons to which it is connected; each neuron can then help store and recall multiple memories (Reber, 2010). Later, when you try to recall a particular memory, that group of neurons fires the same biochemical code associated with it, re-creating the memory in your mind (Mastin, n.d.).

Our initial, immediate memory is short term, lasting only about 30 seconds. It also has limited capacity, as Harvard psychologist and researcher George Miller discovered in the 1950s. Through a series of experiments, he found that our brains can actively focus on and work with approximately seven bits of information at a time (Miller, 1956). The bits of information for what Miller called the Magic Number 7 range from small singular items such as a letter of the alphabet or a single number to chunks of information that the brain is able to group together because of some connection, such as words or mathematical functions.

Try juggling more than seven of these bits at a time, and most of us will begin to mentally stumble and forget some data points, letting some of the information fall to the floor, so to speak (Harvard University Department of Psychology, n.d.). We can thank Miller for our relatively short phone numbers, as it was his research that persuaded phone companies around the world to limit local phone numbers to seven digits. A reexamination of Miller's research (University of South Wales, 2012), however, suggests the magic number may be closer to four, because what we really seem to be doing when we encode a seven-digit number, such as 6458937, is break it into four shorter chunks, such as 64, 58, 93, and 7.

Between four and seven items at a time in our immediate memory—doesn't sound like much, does it? But think about the student activities taking place in your classroom on a daily basis, and you'll see students must constantly employ immediate memory when they are

- Reading a book, a website, or text on a smartboard display and their eyes travel across words in rows. To make sense of the meaning of the

sentences, they have to keep an immediate memory of the previous words they've just read.
- Listening to you or their peers. They use immediate memory to keep track of what's just been said and mentally prepare their responses.
- Working on a math addition or subtraction problem. They have to briefly keep track of place values and carryovers as they solve the calculation.

These initial memories can't get too comfy—this stage lasts only about 30 seconds because, again, the brain must weed out some information. It can't store everything. But if the stimulus is deemed important enough, it can be retained long enough to advance into the next stage, working memory.

Short-Term Working Memory: Up to 20 Minutes

Here's where volition comes in. If we consciously focus on what's in our immediate memory (by listening to someone as they're talking or making marginal notes in a book, for example), we cause our neurons to repeat their chemical and electrical exchanges, which in turn increases the efficiency and strength of their communication (Queensland Brain Institute, n.d.). It's akin to creating a new path through a forest; as your feet press down on the soil and vegetation, it makes the path more visible and easier to follow.

Short-Term Memory Versus Working Memory

For simplicity's sake, this book merges two overlapping yet arguably distinct concepts: short-term memory and working memory. Although cognitive scientists still debate the exact relationship between these ideas (Aben, Stapert, & Bickland, 2012), we might think of the difference like this.

Short-term memory is our stream of consciousness—the sensory events (e.g., listening to a lecture, reading a book) and information (e.g., names, words, numbers) we hold in our attention at any given moment. When we apply mental effort to what's in our short-term memory—for example, manipulating, clustering, or connecting it with stored memories—we employ working memory.

Through brain imaging, scientists have found we appear to activate different parts of our brains when we shift from simply rehashing what's in our short-term memory (e.g., repeating a string of letters) to manipulating what's in short-term memory (e.g., alphabetizing that same string of letters). So we might think of working memory as short-term memory plus mental effort. As we'll see throughout this book, the key to learning almost anything is focusing mental energy on what's in short-term memory—that is, employing working memory. Rather than bouncing back and forth between these two similar ideas, we'll simply use the single, blended term *short-term working memory*.

But it takes more than just one or two walks along the same route in the forest to create an easily seen, easily followed path. Similarly, the pathways in our working memory don't last long, holding on to a recollection roughly 5–20 minutes before the memory either decays or continues its journey to long-term memory.

Although this book mainly focuses on the brain's processing of *new* information, neuroscientists say that our working memory is also used when we activate old memories and bring them front of mind, so to speak. As with the creation of new memories, the more often we recall and think about these existing memories, including combining them with new sensory inputs and information being learned, the more efficient our neural pathways become, strengthening the memories in our minds a bit more each time.

Long-Term Memory: Potentially a Lifetime

If we decide to revisit the information often enough through repetition, rehearsal, contextualization, or application, we can usher it into its ultimate destination. The brain creates more, and larger, dendrites (extensions of the nerve cell) to store these memories (Young, 2015).

Not only that, but activating neurons using different sensory inputs related to the same concepts can strengthen memories and make more connections and pathways between related memories to build broader understanding. In other words, memory and knowledge about a subject—say, civil rights—can be strengthened by reading about civil rights and then also listening to or watching interviews with activists and historians describing what took place and visiting museums or places connected with the civil rights movement.

Effort is everything at this stage; the more we think about and experience a topic, the stronger the memories we create will be. As noted earlier, our brains actively weed out most memories. Researchers think sleep is critical to this process. While we slumber, the subconscious mind sorts and organizes the day's events, embedding the important bits and pieces as best it can and building connections among other related bits and pieces. It also prunes what it regards as useless memories—in particular, memories we haven't stored strongly or connected with other learning. In the morning, we wake up refreshed, ready to load up with a new day's sensory inputs.

Think back to my initial question in the Preface. Can you now sketch out the basics of how memory works—how knowledge enters our brains and is saved for future use?

- Sensory input: We sense something new and our neurons send electrical pulses to our brain.
- Sensory register: Our brain makes a near-instantaneous decision that the sensory data are either important or not important.
- Immediate memory: Important data are processed by the neuron cells in our brains, which create biochemical codes that can re-create the experience later. These codes are shared from neuron to neuron in different parts of the brain, depending on what type of memory is being stored.
- Short-term working memory: If we focus on our immediate memories (or recall prior memories), we can create stronger pathways between our neurons, which increases the likelihood of being able to recall the information later.
- Long-term memory: If we revisit memories to keep the pathways active and add to them by connecting them with other sensory inputs and related memories, we can strengthen our ability to apply old learning to new situations (and vice versa).

This is, of course, a summary of memory formation, and a brief one at that—the equivalent of waterskiing over something we could easily scuba dive into.

Applying Memory Science to a Model for Learning

As we noted earlier, sometimes "brain science" can become too granular and impractical to help educators. We don't really need to know about neuropeptides to be good teachers, but we do need to have solid mental models of how learning occurs so we can use tactics to help our students better seize control of information at just the right time and in the right manner to give that new knowledge the best possible chance for moving through the phases of memory.

So how can we as educators use our knowledge of these phases of information processing to ensure that our lesson planning and instructional delivery help our students' learning stick? By following a learning model, which arranges strategies for teaching and learning into a larger process for helping new knowledge travel through the three types of memory in our students.

Sensory Register and Immediate Memory

We must trigger these two key phases of learning in students' minds for new information to pass through the filters of their sensory registers and enter their immediate memories.

Become interested. The external stimuli that make it past the brain's mental filters tend to be of two varieties: those that stir emotions and those that arouse curiosity (typically in that order). Our brains default to ignoring almost everything else. What this means is that to start the learning process—to get information past our students' mental filters—we need to help them feel comfortable in their learning environment and then attach some form of emotion (e.g., excitement, indignation, passion) and/or intellectual stimulation to what they're learning that leaves them scratching their heads in wonder. For example, we might pose a mystery to them—for example, "Thousands of years ago, the wooly mammoth was the dominant creature in North America. So what happened? How could such a massive creature just up and disappear?"

Commit to learning. Being interested is vital but only gets us so far; to go beyond learning mere tidbits of information or discrete skills, we must take the next step and commit to learning more. As teachers, we can help students do this by presenting new knowledge and skills as part of a big picture that affects their lives and helps them set clear, challenging, yet attainable goals for their learning. In short, when it comes to learning, we need to help students answer the simple question "What's in it for me?" For example, we might help students see how learning why the mammoth went extinct connects to a modern crisis (e.g., the mass extinction of species around the world).

Working Memory

Once information begins tumbling around students' working memories, students must engage in these two phases of learning to begin encoding information, preparing it for long-term memory storage.

Focus on new learning. Once students are "thirsty" for new knowledge, they must acquire it by actively thinking about what they're learning. For example, they might participate in a question-and-answer session, engage in close reading of text, follow a process as it's modeled, visualize what they're learning by creating nonlinguistic representations of concepts, or take notes during a lecture. All these active learning processes, especially when used in combination, help knowledge soak deeper into the brain.

Make sense of learning. Due to the limitations of working memory, we must "chunk" learning into bite-size segments interspersed with opportunities to connect new learning with prior knowledge and cluster ideas together, which is how our brains store knowledge—as webs of ideas and memories. Even though knowledge remains in our working memory, we must "make sense" of it before the details fade. For example, we might help students group various scientific facts, details, and insights into how the wooly mammoth went extinct into three big scientific theories of over-*kill*, over-*ill*, and over-*chill*.

Long-Term Memory

At this point in the process, new learning is still at a crossroads; students' brains are primed to prune the information, discarding it onto a mental trash heap unless they engage in these final two phases of learning.

Practice new learning. To store learning into long-term memory, we must go on more than one date with it, so to speak. As it turns out, cramming seldom works. Rather, we're more apt to remember what we learn when we engage in distributed practice (engaging in practice sessions a few days apart) and retrieval practice (being quizzed on or quizzing ourselves on new knowledge). Learning science shows that searching our memories for knowledge that's begun to fade rekindles those waning neural networks and strengthens memory. Therefore, giving students multiple opportunities to repeat, rehearse, and retrieve new knowledge and skills makes them more apt to commit new learning to memory.

Extend, apply, and find meaning. We've all likely experienced the frustration of struggling to jog our memory for an important bit of information. Often, what's going on in our brains when this happens is that we've stored the information but have too few neural pathways to retrieve it. This "use it or lose it" principle of learning suggests that students more readily retrieve knowledge when they develop multiple connections to it by, for example, associating it with multiple other pieces of information, digging more deeply into it, or using it to solve real-world problems. For example, we might encourage students to delve into the science and ethics of using DNA to bring the wooly mammoth back to life or investigate whether the forces that led to its extinction might now be causing the collapse of global honeybee populations.

Bringing It All Together

In sum, we might visualize this entire process of learning as looking something like Figure 1.1. Together, the steps provide a simple six-phase model for student learning. Figure 1.2 provides more detail about these six phases, along with a practical toolkit for bringing them to life in your classroom that includes

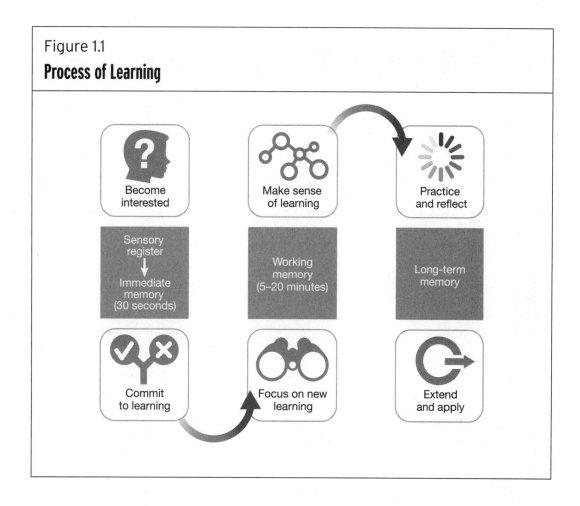

Figure 1.1

Process of Learning

many evidence-based teaching practices from *Classroom Instruction That Works* (Dean et al., 2011) and *The 12 Touchstones of Good Teaching* (Goodwin & Hubbell, 2013). Bear in mind, you needn't use every tool with every lesson but, rather, should use your professional judgment to draw on them to design learning opportunities for your students.

As noted earlier, the labels for each phase of the learning model reflect not what you're doing as a teacher but, rather, what's happening inside students' minds as they learn. Though this may seem like a slight mental and semantic shift, it carries profound significance for how we plan lessons and reflect on and respond to student successes and struggles, which is the essence of professionalism—being able to apply expert knowledge to diagnose and solve problems.

Figure 1.2
Phases of Learning and Classroom Toolkit

Information Processing	Learning Phase	Guiding Questions	Design Principles (learning science)	How Teachers Guide Learning	The Classroom Toolkit
Stimuli in our sensory register catch our attention.	Become interested	Why should students care?	**Emotional valence.** Our brains have a "pecking order" for stimuli; we first pay attention to stimuli with emotional valence.	Prime emotion	• **Show them you care.** Students are more likely to learn if they feel emotionally safe and supported by teachers. • **Connect learning with positive emotions.** Help students connect positive emotions to learning, such as joy, pride, eagerness, and enthusiasm.
		What will spark student interest?	**Curiosity.** After emotionally laden stimuli, our brains attend next to novel stimuli—the unexpected, incomplete, controversial, mysterious, or gaps in our knowledge.	Spark curiosity	• **Spark curiosity.** Use mystery, suspense, or cognitive conflict to hook and hold student interest. • **Activate prior knowledge and reveal knowledge gaps.** Prepare students for learning by helping them recall background knowledge and see gaps in their knowledge. • **Structure academic controversy.** Engage students in debate about content that challenges them cognitively and, as appropriate, emotionally. • **Switch it up.** Infuse learning with novelty and the unexpected to hold students' attention.
We determine whether stimuli are worthy of further attention.	Commit to learning	What meaning will students find?	**Meaning and purpose.** Our limbic (emotional) system is more powerful than our prefrontal (logical) cortex; thus, we must "feel" like learning.	Give a why	• **Give a WIIFM (What's in it for me?).** Students must see why something is important to learn. How will they use it later in life? How do people use it in the real world? • **Frame learning around big ideas/questions.** Students must see the big picture of where learning is headed, so use big ideas/essential questions to guide learning.

Phase	Guiding questions	Concept	Focus	Strategies
	What will motivate students to learn? What will connect them to the learning?	**Connecting to personal interests and goals.** Connecting learning to our own lives motivates and deepens learning. Students are more motivated to learn—and recall later what they've learned—when they set personal goals for learning.	Set learning goals	• **Provide learning objectives and success criteria.** Help students see what's expected—what they're committing to learn—in bite-sized chunks. • **Show students the path to mastery.** Help students see how achieving success criteria will help them achieve their goals by making the path to success transparent, available, and understandable. • **Encourage personal learning goals.** Ensure goals are mastery-, not performance-, oriented. • **Help students commit to effort.** Help students develop an internal locus of control by tracking effort, anticipating roadblocks, and considering how to overcome them.
Focus on new learning	What do I need to show and tell students? How will I help students visualize key concepts?	**Visual learning.** Our brains process information more effectively when it's presented verbally and visually.	Support visual learning	• **Use nonlinguistic representations.** Most of us are visual learners, so visual aids (photos, diagrams, models) support learning, especially if students create them. • **Show and tell.** Illustrating abstract ideas with concrete examples and extracting abstract patterns from concrete examples support learning. • **Model steps to mastery with direct instruction.** Show students the steps for new processes so they see what mastery looks likes (the "I do" phase).
We focus on new knowledge and skills while they're in our working memory.	What do I want students to think about?	**Active engagement.** The only way to keep knowledge in our working memory is to think about it—to actively engage with new knowledge or skills.	Engage in thoughtful learning	• **Alternate worked problems with problems students must solve.** Weaving worked examples into students' own productive struggle boosts processing of new learning (the "we do" phase). • **Teach self-questioning and close reading.** Showing students how to quiz themselves while learning boosts comprehension and retention. • **Engage students in active note taking.** Writing things down (by hand) and drawing pictures enhances memory. Guided notes (filling in blanks) are also effective.

(continued)

Figure 1.2 (continued)

Information Processing	Learning Phase	Guiding Questions	Design Principles (learning science)	How Teachers Guide Learning	The Classroom Toolkit
While new knowledge is in our working memory, we begin to cluster it and link it to prior learning.	Make sense of learning	How will I chunk learning and support information processing?	**Pausing and processing.** Our working memories are limited in how much information they can hold at once (7 ± 2 items) and how long they go before "timing out" (5–20 minutes) and needing to process learning.	Provide time to process	• **"Chunk" learning into segments to support processing.** We must periodically pause during learning to build neural connections. • **Ask probing questions.** Higher-order questions prompt students to think about their learning, apply it, and connect dots with new learning. • **Provide wait time after questions.** Pausing after asking questions and student responses engages more students in thinking about learning and classroom dialogue. • **Use cooperative groups to support processing.** Effective cooperative learning strategies (e.g., reciprocal teaching, classroom dialogue) support processing.
		What themes, categories, sequences, or links to prior learning do students need to make with this learning?	**Categorizing and clustering.** Memories form in our brains as neural networks—as complex webs connecting ideas; in short, we learn by connecting new learning to prior learning.	Help students categorize knowledge	• **Help students identify similarities and differences.** The heart of learning is connecting new ideas to old ones, so comparing, contrasting, and categorizing new learning is essential for making sense of learning. • **Invite students to summarize their learning.** Students are more likely to retain learning when they synthesize and paraphrase what they've learned into big ideas, guiding principles, and key concepts they put into their own words.
Repetition and retrieval help us store new learning in long-term memory.	Practice and reflect	What knowledge and skills must students commit to memory or automate?	**Spaced and interleaved practice.** New learning is more likely to be retained when practice is spaced and reflects "desirable difficulties."	Design and guide deep practice	• **Observe and guide initial practice.** Guidance during initial efforts to apply knowledge or skills ensures students correctly learn procedures and avoid misconceptions. • **Check for understanding.** Identify learning gaps before they become bad habits or misconceptions. • **Provide formative feedback.** Give students nonevaluative descriptive feedback as they learn, helping them reflect on their learning and identify next steps toward mastery.

	Question		Goal	Strategies
Extend and apply Applying new learning in novel, meaningful ways supports retrieval.	What feedback will I provide to guide deep learning?	**Reflecting on gaps in learning or skills.** Repetition that adds new connections to learning along with "discrepancy reduction" enhances storage and retrieval.	Help students reflect on their learning	• **Interleave and space independent practice.** Practicing different skills and spacing out practice sessions support better recall of learning. • **Support frequent retrieval practice.** Straining to recall learning builds retrieval pathways, so ungraded quizzes and other testing devices boost retention of new learning. • **Teach students how to practice.** Show students how to target knowledge and skills they have not yet mastered with interleaving and distributed practice.
	What will I ask students to do with their knowledge?	**Transferring and applying.** Memory storage and retrieval are two different functions; we better retrieve learning when we transfer it to new ways and are more apt to transfer knowledge when we make our thinking visible.	Help students apply learning to new challenges	• **Provide challenging learning tasks.** Help students develop deeper knowledge by engaging them in challenging work that ensures they think about their learning. • **Support inquiry-based learning.** Give students opportunities to explore essential questions via investigations, analyses, and syntheses; without these opportunities, learning quickly fades. • **Make thinking visible.** Thinking aloud when solving problems and explaining their reasoning helps students transfer learning to new situations.
	How will I (and my students) know they've mastered learning?	**Building mental models for critical thinking.** Mental models that integrate declarative and procedural knowledge are essential for deep learning and critical thinking skills. Assessments should engage students in applying mental models and demonstrating critical thinking.	Help students develop mental models and demonstrate deep learning	• **Teach critical thinking.** Contemplating evaluative questions about what they've learned helps students more deeply encode learning. • **Sharpen student thinking with writing.** Writing about learning—in all subject areas—supports deep learning, creating mental models, making meaning, and transferring learning to new situations. • **Anchor learning in performance assessments.** Classrooms assessments often measure only declarative knowledge. Performance assessments ask students to demonstrate both declarative and procedural knowledge while motivating with choice.

We imagine some readers, especially those familiar with *Classroom Instruction That Works*, may wonder how the research-based instructional strategies in that book map onto these phases of learning. Figure 1.3 provides such a link, aligning the 26 strategies from *Classroom Instruction That Works* with the six phases of the learning model offered here. You may note that some strategies, such as questions, align with multiple phases of the model—that's because when skillfully applied, they serve different roles in advancing learning.

Figure 1.3

Mapping *Classroom Instruction That Works* (CITW) onto the Phases of Learning

Learning Phase	Teacher Support	*CITW* Strategies
Become interested	• Hook interest • Activate prior knowledge	• Cues • Advance organizers • Questions
Commit to learning	Help students set goals	• Setting objectives • Reinforcing effort • Providing recognition
Focus on new learning	Provide information	• Pictures and pictographs • Mental images • Note taking • Graphic organizers • Models and manipulatives • Kinesthetic movement
Make sense of learning	Support deeper processing	• Comparing • Questions • Classifying • Cooperative learning • Summarizing
Practice and reflect	Support reflective practice	• Assigning homework • Providing practice • Providing feedback • Reinforcing effort
Extend and apply	Support deeper learning and application	• Questions • Problem solving • Experimental inquiry • Systems analysis • Investigation

As you'll soon discover, these six phases are also based on the assumption that intrinsic motivation—not external punishments and rewards—is the true key to deeper learning. After all, when you think about it, all learning (with the possible exceptions of brainwashing or subliminal advertising) requires the learner to be a willing participant in the process. Although we can cajole, bribe, or bird-dog, we really cannot force anyone to learn anything. In the end, learning only occurs when the learner decides (or relents) to learning something.

Most of the meaningful things we learn in life, in fact—whether it's our native tongue, a hobby, or the lyrics of our favorite song—we learned because we saw the value of learning and often experienced joy in doing so. With that in mind, a key idea that runs through all six phases of learning is that intellectual curiosity—the need to explore, answer questions, and encounter new experiences—is the best companion to learning.

We'll start the next chapter with this idea—how curiosity can spark learning—and return to it repeatedly, showing you how to design learning experiences for your students that tap into what lies deep inside them: an innate desire to learn. In so doing, you'll be able to create learning experiences for your students that tap into and unleash their curiosity, making the entire process of learning easier and more joyful for both you and your students.

2

Become Interested

According to media reports, a trend among hip urbanites from Brooklyn to San Francisco is doing absolutely nothing—that is, spending an hour or more in a sensory deprivation chamber. Apparently, for many people who feel overstimulated by the constant chirping of smartphones, nonstop media, and ubiquitous screens demanding our attention in restaurants, elevators, and the backs of plane seats, the best respite has become immersing oneself in a saltwater tank in utter silence and darkness.

As Nathan Heller (2017) shared in *Vogue* magazine, the experience—floating in the dark in warm salt water so he felt, heard, and saw nothing—was disorienting at first, and his "mind began to behave like a hammy actor in an empty theater" engaged in a melodramatic loop of observations and anxieties. But after it calmed down, Heller recalled early childhood experiences in vivid detail, like his grandparents making peach gelatin using ice cubes. Heller emerged from the experience feeling refreshed; the whole experience "had done what I had hoped: I'd found a way of rediscovering my mind."

For some, though, sensory deprivation in a saltwater tank can become a nightmarish experience. Allison Davis (2015), for example, found that the experience rubbed salt in open wounds (literally), made her feel nauseous to the point she thought she might be dying, and spurred the fear that she might contract sepsis (all while wondering, "What is sepsis, even?"). Her brain, unmoored from its senses, began spinning in "a jumble of *death-barf-panic-what-is-sepsis* thoughts."

Living and Learning in an Era of Sensory Overload

What these experiences reveal is how accustomed our brains are to being bombarded with sensory input. Our senses reportedly relay 11 million bits of information per second to our brains, which can process, at most, only about 120 bits per second (Levitin, 2015). To understand someone talking to us, for example, our brains must process about 60 bits of information per second, which explains why it's difficult to listen to two people talking at once (and impossible to listen to three simultaneously); we simply cannot squeeze 180 bits of information into a 120-bit mental pipe (Levitin, 2015).

Modern life, though, forces us to operate during most waking hours at close to maximum information processing capacity. According to one now-likely underestimate by researchers at the University of Southern California (Hilbert & Lopez, 2011), people receive the equivalent of 174 newspapers (of 85 pages each) of information every day—a fivefold increase from just 20 years earlier. All of this information processing and filtering takes a toll. That's because our brains require enormous amounts of glucose and oxygen to operate. So, just like any other part of our bodies, they become fatigued and "have trouble separating the trivial from the important," especially when they're overtaxed (Levitin, 2015, n.p.).

Cognitive scientist and writer Daniel Goleman (2013) has observed that this difficulty is especially true for a new generation of students: "Today's children are growing up in a new reality, one where they are attuning more to machines and less to people than has ever been true in human history" (p. 6). He argues this trend is "troubling for several reasons" (p. 6), including that it appears to impair many students' ability to pay attention. As a teacher told Goleman, "It's hard to teach comma rules when you are competing with *World of Warcraft*" (p. 7).

Learning doesn't happen through osmosis, of course. So if students are to learn anything, they must first pay attention to it. That means today's teachers must be increasingly adept at capturing students' interest long enough to draw their often-overloaded minds into the quieter process of learning.

The Toll of Emotional Turmoil on Attention

In addition to getting and holding students' attention, we must also design learning experiences that reflect the reality of our brain laid bare in sensory deprivation tanks; namely, that our minds are rarely quiet but instead constantly churning with ideas, words, memories, and emotions—something commonly referred to as our "stream of consciousness." In the darkened silence of a sensory deprivation tank, it often becomes apparent—painfully so to some—that in addition to processing external stimuli, our brains expend a great deal of energy chewing on prior experiences and, in particular, those experiences associated with strong emotions.

That's why prior to entering a sensory deprivation chamber, users are often urged to clear their minds of negative emotions and anxieties, as both are often heightened when our brains have nothing else (or at least no external stimuli) to process. This phenomenon reveals another fundamental truth: we pay attention to not only external stimuli in the sensory register but also internal stimuli already present in our emotions, experiences, and stream of consciousness.

For many students, especially those who are experiencing chronic stress (often the result of adverse childhood experiences), these internal stimuli may pose particular challenges to paying attention in class. An examination of data for some 100,000 students across the United States (Bethell, Newacheck, Hawes, & Halfon, 2014), for example, found that 48 percent under the age of 17 have endured a least one adverse childhood experience (including exposure to violence; emotional, physical, or sexual abuse; deprivation, neglect, or social discrimination; family discord or divorce; parental substance abuse, mental health problems, death, or incarceration), and 22.6 percent have had more than one adverse childhood experience. Neuroscience has found that people with post-traumatic stress, which includes children who have experienced one or more adverse childhood experience, have a smaller hippocampus—the region of the brain responsible for converting short-term to long-term memories (Bremner, 2006). In addition, studies have found that people with post-traumatic stress disorder (PTSD) register increased activity in their amygdala, which triggers fight-or-flight responses and decreased activity in their medial prefrontal cortex, which helps tamp down anxiety.

In other words, exposure to intense psychological distress can leave students in a constant state of high alert that makes it difficult for them to concentrate. It also appears to contribute to deficits in verbal declarative memory—the very stuff, of course, of most academic learning. For these reasons, students with adverse childhood experiences may appear irritable or distractible, or they may struggle to retain new knowledge in classrooms (Streeck-Fischer & van der Kolk, 2000).

Our Brains' "Pecking Order" for Processing Stimuli

A key takeaway from all this for teachers is that for learning to occur, new learning must first cut through the clutter of students' sensory registers and the constant churn of internal emotions, ideas, and thoughts they bring to the classroom. How can teachers do this? A starting point is to consider how students' brains filter the millions of bits of information streaming into them each second down to a tiny pinhole of 120 or so bits of information per second worth paying attention to. In general, the filtering process reflects this pecking order:

- **Emotional valence.** Our brains tend to pay attention first to stimuli that stir strong emotions—that are very pleasant/attractive or very unpleasant/unattractive. Threats to our personal health and safety are high on the list. This seems only natural. After all, if our ancestors couldn't quickly focus on the presence of threats, such as a snake in the grass coiled and ready to strike, it would have been lights out for our species. Tuning into appealing stimuli also makes sense; focusing on finding food, dry shelter, and potential mates had other obvious survival and evolutionary benefits.
- **Novelty.** Our brains also tend to pay attention to new (and dynamic) objects, people, and ideas in our environment (and disregard old or static ones). Our senses are drawn to strange sights, sounds, and smells, like attending to rustling in the brush behind us. Basically, our brains quickly disregard familiar stimuli (a tree we've passed many times before) as being of little consequence to help us focus on important changes in our environment (e.g., *Hey, there's a ripe mango in that tree that wasn't there before*).
- **Curiosity.** After emotional and novel stimuli, our brains are drawn next to perplexing stimuli—puzzles, mysteries, and things in our environment that fill us with wonder or contradict our expectations (e.g., *That family in the cave next to us made a fire. How did they do that?*). As cognitive scientist John Medina (2008) notes, curiosity is deeply ingrained in all of us and is evident even in very young children who demonstrate a natural desire to explore their environments, crawling from room to room and putting things in their mouths, which creates a need to "baby-proof" our homes and, at times, wash off the dog's chew toy so we can give it back to the dog.

Become Interested: A Classroom Toolkit

By understanding—and tapping into—the pecking order students' brains apply to their sensory registers, teachers can help students—even those with sensory overload or who may be feeling emotionally distraught—become interested in learning. Here are some critical strategies to build into learning experiences. As noted earlier, you should view these strategies as a toolkit; you don't necessarily need to apply every strategy for every unit or lesson. Rather, see them as go-to strategies for building students' interest in what they're learning.

Show Them You Care

Perhaps the most important takeaway from this research is that in order to learn, students must feel physically and emotionally safe. If students' minds are preoccupied with concern about their health and safety, it will be difficult (if not impossible) for their brains to allow other stimuli, such as your great lesson on meteorology or chemical reactions, into their sensory register. Students who are dealing with traumatic situations at home (domestic violence, homelessness, poverty) or in school (bullying) have an understandably difficult time setting those events aside and focusing on learning what you're teaching.

In *The 12 Touchstones of Good Teaching* (Goodwin & Hubbell, 2013), we described such an environment as an "oasis of safety and respect," recognizing that many students live in a "desert" of meaningful adult and interpersonal interactions. Our job as teachers is to reassure students that regardless of what else may be going on in their lives, inside the walls of our classrooms (where we're in charge), they'll be treated with kindness and respect.

Studies actually support the power of creating such environments. For example, a meta-analysis of 119 studies with data from more than 300,000 students found that teacher empathy and warmth were linked not only to better behavior and motivation but also to higher levels of achievement (Cornelius-White, 2007). Other studies have found that kindergarten students who developed positive relationships with their teachers were more likely to demonstrate better behavior and higher achievement in subsequent grades (Hamre & Pianta, 2001). For at-risk students, in particular, teachers' instructional practices are less important to students' success than the level of emotional support they receive from their teachers (Hamre & Pianta, 2005).

Older students also benefit from classrooms that provide emotional and psychological safety. For example, middle school students whose teachers showed they cared about them as individuals were three times more likely be engaged in school, whereas middle schoolers with low levels of emotional support from teachers were 68 percent more likely to be disengaged from school (Klem & Connell, 2004).

Given what we know about the brain's sensory register, these findings are hardly surprising. The learning process is unlikely to begin if students' minds are churning with unpleasant emotions and memories, leaving them unable to attend to the learning at hand. How can we show students we care and provide them with emotional safety? Here are few guiding principles to keep in mind:

- **Provide positivity.** Recall that our brains are most apt to register stimuli laden with positive emotions. That means if your classroom is a positive place, filled with joy, optimism, and genuine concern for students, students are more apt to open their filters. Here's a small proof point: a study of 104 college students (Frederickson & Branigan, 2005) found that when students watched films that elicited positive emotions (e.g., tenderness or optimism), they demonstrated a broader range of attention and greater openness to new knowledge, contemplation, and effort than students shown films that elicited negative emotions (e.g., anger or anxiety).
- **Be a warm demander.** Years ago, Judith Kleinfeld (1972) identified a group of positive outlier teachers whose capacity to hold high expectations for learning while creating strong, positive relationships with their students (many Native Alaskan) fostered significantly higher levels of success than other teachers.
- **Be present.** Teachers need to be an active, dynamic presence in the classroom. A key differentiator of effective teachers is something Jacob Kounin (1970) captured nicely in a term he coined years ago—*withitness*—that refers to a teacher's ability to fill a classroom, have "eyes in the back of their head," and be aware of what's going on in all spaces of the classroom at all times. Withitness provides emotional safety not by pouncing on misdeeds but by rewarding positive behaviors and redirecting potentially negative interactions among students to help everyone feel safe.
- **Create shared agreements for kindness and respect.** Studies have shown that positive peer pressure is often the best means to create safe and supportive classroom environments (Smith & Fowler, 1984). Thus, one of the best ways to create a peaceful, supportive classroom environment is to engage students in developing rules for classroom behavior that are framed in the positive (e.g., "We take turns," "We engage in active listening").

The point here is that we've long known that learning falls well down the list of human needs, according to psychologist Abraham Maslow (1954). That means that in order for students to learn, they must first feel safe and accepted. If, as teachers, we plunge directly into teaching and skip right past these basic human needs for students, those who feel unsafe or insecure will be unlikely to learn.

Try This: 2 by 10

If you're struggling to connect with a student, agree to meet two minutes per day for 10 days to talk about anything the student wants. These conversations are meant to be unconditional; that is, they are not a punishment or reward (or withheld if the student has bad behavior). It's an opportunity for you to form a stronger bond with a student, showing them you care (Curwin et al., 2018).

Connect Learning with Positive Emotions

Brain science tells us that we tend to pay more attention to stimuli with emotional valence and that our more primitive limbic brains—home to emotions and unconscious responses to our environment—are far more powerful than our more sophisticated prefrontal cortexes, which are home to logic and conscious thought. Social psychologist and researcher Johnathan Haidt (2006) created the metaphor of an elephant and rider to describe how these parts of our brains interact with one another. Our logical, conscious brain wants to think it's in charge, but it is a mere rider atop an elephant of emotions and unconscious, reflexive reactions. Sometimes, the rider controls the elephant, but for the most part, the elephant pretty much goes where it wants to go—with the rider later justifying actions and feelings. What this suggests is that we must feel like doing something before we do it, including learning.

Studies have found, in fact, that we're more apt to recall learning that's attached to positive emotions, which appear to serve as hooks for later recalling what we've learned (Isen, Daubman, & Nowicki, 1987; Isen, Shalker, Clark, & Karp, 1978). A small randomized control trial with college students (Um, Plass, Hayward, & Homer, 2012) offers a case in point. One group of students engaged in a bland, black-and-white version of lessons on how immunization works and read neutral (i.e., boring) statements between learning segments (e.g., "There are 60 minutes in an hour," "Apples are harvested in the fall"). The other group engaged in full-color versions of the lessons complete with cute animated characters and read aloud positive statements such as "It doesn't get any better than this!" and "It's great to be alive!" Afterward, researchers concluded that students in the positive emotion group focused more on learning, found the materials easier to comprehend, and did better on a follow-up test.

We know from research (Dean et al., 2012) that two of the most powerful teaching strategies we can employ are (1) providing students with cues—hints at the outset of a lesson about where a lesson is going that connect what students know with what they will learn, and (2) advanced organizers—stories, pictures, and other introductory materials to help students focus on the new learning. You can connect these dots in your classroom by providing cues and advance organizers for your lessons and units that invoke positive emotions (e.g., joy, hope, wonder, inspiration, enthusiasm, compassion, satisfaction, affection). Here are a few examples:

- Have you ever done something that took a few seconds of "insane courage" to do but afterward made you feel proud? Like jumping off a high dive? Or talking to a famous person? Today, we're going to learn about someone who helped change our society with an act of insane courage: sitting in the front seat of a bus.
- Last week, we really challenged our brains by multiplying two-digit numbers. Afterward, I know you all felt proud showing me you could do some really tough math. Because you all did so well with that, I think you're up to an even bigger challenge—this one is going to be like fighting the "boss" at the end of a video game. So are you ready for some super-challenging math?
- I imagine you all have a soft spot in your heart for someone—maybe it's a friend, family member, or someone you work with who allows you to see things in them that others don't see. Great writers do the same thing. They often develop characters that are flawed or imperfect but still have great affection for them—and they want us to see that goodness in them, too. I won't tell you who it is right now, but you're going to find a character like that in John Steinbeck's *Of Mice and Men*.

It's worth noting that not all learning must (or can) be tied to emotions, especially if doing so becomes an off-task distraction. Studies have found, for example, that adding interesting but ultimately unimportant elements to texts can hamper students' ability to learn the main points of the text (Moreno & Mayer, 2000). Bottom line: use emotional hooks when they're a natural fit for what you want students to learn.

Spark Curiosity

As a teacher, it can be easy to fall into a pattern of adopting a "just the facts, ma'am" approach to teaching—introducing content in a straightforward manner for the sake of efficiency. However, when we just blandly share information or concepts with students without helping them become interested in it, we rob them of the wonder of discovery, which, after all, is at the heart of learning. One of the most powerful ways to capture student interest is to tap into their natural sense of curiosity. Studies over a few decades (Loewenstein, 1994) identified and tested several conditions that arouse curiosity—conditions you can create in your classroom to grab student interest. Here are a few of them.

Mystery. Knowing that someone knows something we don't arouses curiosity. We might also call this the "I have a secret" phenomenon. For example, a friend telling you she bought a present for you but won't tell you what it is until your birthday or hearing someone sitting next to you chuckling while reading a magazine is likely to arouse your curiosity. Years ago, Robert Cialdini (2005), a psychologist at Arizona State University, wrote an article titled "What's the Secret Device for Engaging Student Interest? Hint: The Answer Is in the Title." In it, he shared how he sifted through dozens of science articles to figure how to make complex content more interesting for students. He found that the best science writers eschew the typical, yawn-inducing opener "In this article, I will present arguments in favor of my theory of XYZ" and instead pose questions such as "What are the rings of Saturn made of? Rock or ice?" Throughout the article, they build suspense about their topic—arguments in favor of rock and ice—before resolving the mystery in the end. (The answer, in this case, is both.)

Cognitive conflict. Curiosity also emerges when we encounter something that doesn't fit our expectations. Consider, for example, the spark of curiosity you likely feel when you learn (or learned) that winds blowing down from chilly mountaintops into valleys below are warm, not cold, or that offering supermarket shoppers five or six choices of jams, as opposed to dozens, encourages them to buy more jam. In both cases, you may find yourself wondering, "Why is that?"

A small study (Baser, 2006) put this idea to the test by engaging student groups in learning about the concept in physics of heat transfer (i.e., heat transfers through conduction, convection, or radiation). The first group learned about the concept the "usual" way: a teacher lectured on the concept, provided an equation for heat transfer, showed students how to work problems with the equation, and answered some questions. The second group, however, experienced cognitive conflict; students were asked whether they thought the metal legs or vinyl cushions of their desks were warmer. Most assumed the vinyl until a thermometer showed both were the same temperature even though the metal felt cooler to the touch. The rest of the lesson focused on students' questions about the topic (e.g., "Our sensation tells us something, and we know that it may not be temperature. So what is the thing we sense?"). Afterward, a test revealed that students in the second cognitive conflict group had gained significantly better understanding of the concept of heat transfer than the first group.

Suspense. We're also suckers for incomplete sequences (e.g., "1, 2, 3, 5, 8—what comes next?") and unfinished narratives (e.g., a cliff-hanger prior to a commercial break). Riddles and puzzles also fit into this category. However, it's important to note what psychologists refer to as a "reference-point" phenomenon—that is, curiosity depends on prior knowledge (Loewenstein, 1994, p. 87). We must know something about a topic first to be curious about it. This phenomenon explains why you're probably more curious, for example, about the nocturnal habits of your housecat than of an African serval. It also explains why we tend to become more interested in a topic when we see the gap in our knowledge getting smaller. For example, it's much harder to put down a mystery novel five pages from the ending than five pages from the beginning. Here are a few examples of cliff-hangers you can use in your classroom.

- We've seen that Ralph and Jack have very different personalities. They're both leaders, yet there's some tension brewing between them. What do you think will happen now that the boys are alone on the island?
- We know that mixing baking soda and vinegar together creates carbon dioxide. What do you think will happen when we place this mixture near a lit candle?
- We've seen the complex alliances that formed across Europe in the early 20th century. How do you think these nations will respond if a leader of one nation is assassinated?

Guessing and receiving feedback. The flip side of a reference-point phenomenon is being aware of our knowledge gaps—overcoming what we might call a "fat but happy" syndrome in which we think we know more about something than we actually do. Studies have shown that one way to overcome this syndrome and come to grips with our information gaps is to receive "accuracy feedback"—that is, to make a guess and learn we have guessed wrong. For example, in one experiment (Loewenstein, 1994), researchers found that subjects were more interested to learn the easternmost state in the United States after having the opportunity to guess (and receive feedback) on the westernmost state in the nation (i.e., Alaska, which, as it turns out, crosses the international dateline, making it both the westernmost and easternmost state in the nation).

Activate Prior Knowledge and Reveal Knowledge Gaps

A key concept from the science of learning is a rather simple one: "All new learning requires a foundation of prior knowledge" (Brown et al., 2014, p. 5). Basically, it's difficult, if not impossible, to learn something you know nothing about. That's why universities require students to take prerequisite courses before taking advanced-level courses. It's also why one of the most effective teaching strategies is helping students recall their prior knowledge and draw connections to it as they build new knowledge (Bransford & Johnson, 1972).

For example, a scientific study of 6th and 7th graders asked half the group to engage in "elaborative interrogation" (i.e., drawing on prior knowledge to explain why a particular science fact might be true) while reading several statements about science facts and the other half to carefully "read the statements for meaning." Afterward, the researchers found that students who consciously activated their prior knowledge with elaborative interrogation while reading the statements demonstrated significantly better recall of the statements when tested on them later—gains that remained a full six months later (Woloshyn, Paivio, & Pressley, 1994).

This concept suggests one of the most important things you can do as a teacher is to invite your students to share, recall, or brainstorm what they already know about a topic they are going to learn more about—doing so primes their brains for learning. Next, you can help them see what they *don't* know about a topic and in so doing arouse their curiosity. That's because the heart of all curiosity is becoming aware of—and then wanting to close—a gap in our knowledge. Basically, our brains hate knowledge gaps and want to close them. Yet if we perceive a knowledge gap is too great for us to close, we're less likely to engage in learning—as a study of 400 middle, high school, and university students found (Gentry et. al, 2002): students who reported having large gaps between what they knew and what they wanted to know at the beginning of the semester were prone to learned helplessness and lower academic performance by the end of the term.

Here are some ways you can activate students' prior knowledge, while helping them recognize new gaps in their knowledge—often by employing a variant of the "you know this, but did you know that" sentence stem:

- You've learned about Jamestown and Plymouth Bay, but did you know that years before either of these colonies, another one was founded—and disappeared?

- You know that most poems contain rhymes, but did you know that some poems don't rhyme at all? Or use words that sort of rhyme but actually don't?
- We've learned how to solve problems with the quadratic formula, but did you know we can use the quadratic formula to solve all kinds of real-world problems?

Structure Academic Controversy

Researchers have also found that controversy begets curiosity (which may explain the prevalence of dueling pundits on cable news shows). There's a tendency, of course, in the highly politicized environment of public schools to avoid controversial topics (e.g., evolution, climate change, political debates) altogether. However, research on curiosity would suggest that instead of avoiding or glossing over the thorny elements of such controversies, we should actually use the controversy to teach students.

In a now-famous experiment, Lowry and Johnson (1981) randomly assigned 5th and 6th grade students to work in groups. One group was instructed to engage in a cooperative learning about a particular topic (e.g., strip mining or designating wolves as endangered species); the other was encouraged to focus on controversy in the topic. Students in the controversy condition demonstrated more interest in the topic, sought more information on it, and were more likely to give up a recess period to watch a film about it.

Here are few ways you can use structured academic controversy to tap into student curiosity:

- Identify an issue with differing positions. Pose a question to encourage students to think deeply about the issue. Challenge students to research various views of the issue, identify the viewpoint closest to their own, and defend it.
- Assign groups of students to different sides of a controversial issue or historical argument (e.g., Should the U.S. colonies declare independence? Should we ban plastic straws?). Ask student groups to research the issue, develop respective viewpoints (and counterarguments to the view of other groups), and stage a structured classroom debate.
- Ask students to identify a controversy in history, literature, science, current affairs, or their own lives and write an argumentative essay from both

points of view—applying the same rubric for thesis statements, supporting details, and cogent arguments to both essays.

Switch It Up

Readers of a certain age will likely remember the old television commercials for Dunkin' Donuts in which "Fred the Baker" says, repetitiously, every morning as his alarm sounds and he staggers out the door before dawn, "Time to make the donuts." In hindsight, I'm not really sure what the point of those ads were, but I can still recall how as a young teacher, my colleague and roommate and I used to jokingly mutter that line as we carpooled to school in the morning.

Fred, I think, found joy in baking donuts, but sometimes, for him as well as us teachers, it can be easy to fall into a rut of feeling like we're doing the same thing every day. And if we're feeling that way, it's dead certain our students are, too. Moreover, if our classrooms are falling into familiar ruts and routines, it's likely our students' brains will be telling them that what's happening in our class is of little consequence—*Been there, done that*, their brains will say. *No need to pay attention.*

Knowing that our students' brains are attuned to novel stimuli suggests we, too, need to switch things up from time to time, doing something unexpected at the start or the middle of a lesson. For example, we might bring a conch shell and invite students to pass it to one another during a class on *The Lord of the Flies*. Or we might ask students to turn their desks toward the west for a class on westward expansion, or purposefully make blundering mistakes when solving math problems to see if students are paying attention.

Recall, too, that the human brain is an amazingly energy-intensive organ, so it's quick to power down. Keeping students' brains focused on learning requires effort and a lot of energy. In fact, after about 10 minutes of engaging in the same stimulus, its novelty will begin to fade. As a result, students (and adults, for that matter) tend to check out mentally after about 10 minutes unless something happens to reengage them in the learning task at hand. As cognitive scientist John Medina (2008) writes, to keep students interested in learning, we need to "keep grabbing them back by telling narratives or creating events rich in emotion" (p. 111).

One way to do this, suggested by Douglas Lemov (2010), is to put a little "Vegas" or "sparkle in a lesson" to keep students interested. This doesn't mean providing razzle-dazzle for its own sake or engaging in a lengthy, time-wasting diversion from learning, but rather something closely related to what you want students to learn. For example, it might "be a 30 second break to do the 'action verb shimmy'" or "a brief competition to see who can do the best charade for the day's vocabulary word" (p. 141).

The science of learning, in fact, suggests that students are more apt to recall what they've learned when they can link it to some novel stimuli. For example, as we'll discuss in more detail in the chapter on practicing and rehearsing new learning, we're more likely to recall information we've learned in many different places, instead of just one. So, by creating novelty in your classroom, you'll not only grab students' interest by triggering their brains to pay attention, but also give them more mental hooks to recall what they've learned later.

The Big Idea: Accelerating Learning by Unleashing Students' Natural Curiosity

As educators, the good news we might extract from this research on curiosity is that while our brains are often hamster wheels of external stimuli and churning internal thoughts, they nonetheless crave exploring, solving puzzles, and paying attention to interesting stimuli in our environment. Simply stated, human beings are naturally curious. Indeed, as any parent of a toddler will tell you, children are full of questions—lots of them—which is to say, they're naturally disposed to learning.

Yet by the time they reach school age, their questions come fewer and farther between. Researchers have observed, for example, that toddlers ask up to 100 questions per day, but by middle school, that number dwindles to virtually nil (Bronson & Merryman, 2010)—not because kids themselves become less curious but because, as numerous studies have found, school and classroom conditions often drain their curiosity (Engel, 2015).

Consider for a moment, how the previous list of curiosity-creating conditions contrasts with typical classroom environments:

- How often do teachers call out puzzling incongruities in what they're teaching in, say, world history (e.g., that nearly one-third of the time when a small nation goes to war against a larger one, the small nation wins) versus simply laboring through content?
- How often do we gloss over controversy in history, economics, or science, instead of using it as a vehicle for student engagement? Like Ben Stein's

teacher character in *Ferris Bueller's Day Off*, how often do we simply *tell* students about the Laffer curve rather than give them the opportunity to dive into the controversial concept?

• How often do we write the learning objective in front of the room and direct students to dutifully learn it versus turning our classrooms—and students' learning objectives—into mysteries they earnestly want to solve?

It's not hard to see that often what we do in many classrooms runs almost entirely counter to what we know from research about sparks curiosity. Nor is it surprising, then, that researchers have found that the longer children stay in school, the less curiosity they demonstrate. For example, through her series of classroom observations, Susan Engel (2015) found kindergarten students display on average 2.36 episodes of curiosity over a two-hour period. By 5th grade, that number drops to 0.48 episodes in a two-hour period, which suggests that many children spend their entire school day "without asking even one question or engaging in one sequence of behavior aimed at finding out something new" (Engel, 2011, p. 633).

At issue, Engel has observed, is that many teachers feel pressured to cover material and thus have "very specific objectives for each stretch of time" and "put a great deal of effort into keeping children on task and reaching those objectives" (2011, p. 636). As a result, they tend not only to gloss over curiosity as an important spark for learning but also to treat student questions and curiosity not as teachable moments but as off-task distractions.

Unleashing student curiosity takes time—something many teachers often feel is in short supply when facing an externally mandated press to cover content. Yet if we can tap into student curiosity—while ensuring students feel emotionally safe and ready to learn—we can create classrooms that spark their curiosity and, in the process, make learning a whole lot easier, more enjoyable, and more effective and efficient. In short, by taking the time to help students become interested in what they are learning, we can accelerate the entire process of learning.

In the next chapter, we'll explore how to leverage students' initial interest in new learning by helping them commit to learning and, in so doing, take new learning deeper into their immediate and working memories.

3

Commit to Learning

Most teachers probably have at least one "brussels sprouts" unit: a required part of the curriculum they find less than enjoyable to teach. For me (with apologies to Nathaniel Hawthorne fans), it was *The Scarlet Letter*. My own dispassion rubbed off on my students. They were forever asking why they must read something so *boring*. I haplessly tried to convince them it was an important literary work that offered insights into Puritan influence on U.S. culture, but my own explanations were half-hearted. Deep down, the only reason I was teaching the book was because my curriculum guide said I must.

As it turns out, my 14- and 15-year-old high school students had likely progressed far into what child psychologist Jean Piaget (1972) long ago characterized as *formal operations*—when students begin to think more abstractly and metacognitively, which includes asking an all-important question: *Why must I learn this?* When teachers fail to answer that question satisfactorily, student engagement suffers.

Turning Boredom into Commitment

Boredom in high school isn't a new phenomenon, of course, yet current data suggest that many, if not most, high school students are bored out of their minds—though it's important to note that most don't start their academic careers that way. For example, a 2013 Gallup poll of 500,000 students from 5th to 12th grade found that roughly 8 in 10 elementary students felt "engaged" in school—that is, attentive, curious, and optimistic about their learning. Yet among 11th graders, that number had been cut in half—with just 4 in 10 feeling engaged (Busteed, 2013). When Gallup asked teenagers in 2004 to select 3 adjectives from a list of 14 to describe how they usually feel in school, the top choices were *bored* (selected by 50 percent of students) and *tired* (selected by 42 percent). Only 2 percent said they were never bored (Lyons, 2004).

Let that soak in for a moment. At the very age school experiences ought to be exposing students to the mysteries of science, the drama of human history, the elegant language of mathematics, and great works of literature, they are bored out of their minds. Why should that be?

Helping Students Find Meaning and Purpose in Learning

Harvard professor Jal Mehta, who spent several years studying student motivation and engagement, notes that many students simply see no value in what they're learning. "There's no big external motivating force in American education except for the fraction of kids who want to go to the most selective colleges," he told Harvard's *Ed. Magazine* (Jason, 2017, p. 20).

Not all so-called boredom is bad, of course. At some point, learning something in depth requires powering through some form of repetition or focused effort. Musicians, for example, must learn chords and scales, tennis players must serve bucket after bucket of tennis balls, and writers must master grammatical rules. The point here is that if students are committed to mastering a new set of skills or knowledge, they won't begrudge but rather embrace the repetition and focused effort.

Indeed, as Mihaly Csikszentmihalyi and colleagues found in a study of talented teenagers—those who nurtured their talents (academic, athletic, and artistic) through dedicated hard work and effort—these students had identified for themselves a deeper purpose to propel their efforts: to become a professional musician, achieve success in sports, or pursue mathematics at a competitive university (Csikszentmihalyi, Rathunde, & Whalen, 1993). They had committed to learning because they could see value for themselves in what they were learning.

Convincing the Brain to "Power Up" and Learn Something New

When you think about it, we don't tend to learn anything without, at some point, committing to learning it. That's because all learning requires what cognitive scientist Daniel Kahneman (2011) describes as "effortful thinking." As Kahneman explains it, our brains essentially have two operating systems: a fast-thinking brain, which operates quickly and automatically with little thought, often because it's employing prior learning that has become automated;

and a slow-thinking brain, which requires attention and gets easily interrupted when our attention is diverted.

Our slow-thinking brain is generally in charge, but according to Kahneman, "one of its main characteristics is laziness, a reluctance to invest more effort than is strictly necessary" (p. 31). Acquiring new knowledge and skills, however, requires our brains to maintain focused attention, process information, and reflect on learning—mental functions that all require intense effort and energy. As a result, our brains constantly want to slide back into low-effort mode and basically avoid learning and other forms of effortful thinking.

What this means is that to learn, we must convince our brains it's worth the effort to stay powered up. We must tell our brains we *want* to learn something (e.g., because we find it fascinating), *need* to learn something (e.g., because we find it useful), or *should* learn something (e.g., because it will help someone else).

Such commitment to learning tells our brains to pay attention to something in our sensory register so it can enter our immediate memory and keep us focused long enough to leave an impression on our working memory. For example, if we decide to commit to learning how to hit a tennis topspin because we're convinced it will make us a better tennis player, we're more likely to focus on our tennis coach, listen to her explanation for how to hit a topspin, and watch her closely as she models the process, swinging her racket in an upward motion to put spin on the ball. If we lack such volition or commitment (e.g., telling ourselves, *I think tennis is dumb*), learning is unlikely to occur because our brains will simply slip back into low-effort mode (e.g., *I'll use my racket to play air guitar*).

In his synthesis of research on student motivation, Jere Brophy (2004) boils decades of research on student engagement down to a simple formula: *expectancy × value.* That is, for students to commit to learning, they need some expectation they can be successful in learning it (e.g., *I can picture myself hitting a topspin*) and also be able to see value in its outcome (e.g., *Keeping the ball in the court while hitting it harder will help me win matches*). If students don't value what they're being asked to learn, they tend to react with frustration and anger, which itself creates cognitive strain and redirects mental energies to thinking about how much they resent being coerced into learning something (Brophy, 2004).

Balancing Extrinsic and Intrinsic Rewards

As teachers, we essentially have two ways to motivate students to commit to learning: external rewards (e.g., gold stars, pizza parties, grades) and internal rewards (e.g., tapping into their innate curiosity, desire to learn, and joy of discovery). A common go-to strategy for motivating students has largely been the former.

As many teachers have no doubt discovered, these carrot-and-stick approaches can be effective—but only to a point. As Alfie Kohn (1999) observed, the net effect of these approaches is that over time, students come to view learning not as something they actually want to do but as something they must do if they want to have candy or go to the playground. For example, when researchers gave young children cookies for drawing pictures (something they were doing for enjoyment prior to the study), those students were less likely to entertain themselves by drawing pictures afterward, presumably because those rewards had turned the erstwhile fun activity of drawing into a chore—something done to please others, not themselves (Deci, Ryan, & Koestner, 1999).

So, if we bribe students for doing what they ought to find naturally rewarding (i.e., learning), we may inadvertently send the message that learning is an unpleasant chore. And if our entire system for motivating students is based on external motivators—such as grades, gold stars, report cards, and extra homework for bad behavior—we be may be sending the message that this whole enterprise of learning is a kind of unpleasantness to be endured.

Moreover, carrots and sticks are effective in motivating only certain kinds of behavior on certain kinds of tasks, as a meta-analysis of 40 years of research confirmed (Cerasoli, Nicklin, & Ford, 2014). It found that both extrinsic and intrinsic rewards motivate behavior, but extrinsic rewards are more effective for motivating performance on simpler and less inherently enjoyable tasks, and intrinsic rewards are more powerful for motivating performance on more engaging and complex tasks.

In other words, if you want your kid to mow the lawn, an extrinsic reward (like $10) is probably the best incentive. But if you want your grass cut in perfectly straight rows with hand-clipped edges so your lawn resembles the infield of a major league baseball park, you'll likely need to foster intrinsic motivation in your teen (e.g., a deep appreciation of lawn care and burning desire to show up the neighbors)—or perhaps just do it yourself.

With all of this in mind, the guiding principles for helping students commit to learning offered here skew toward fostering an intrinsic motivation to learn—helping students tell their brains, "Hey, pay attention because I want to/need to/should learn this because it is fascinating/useful/helpful/important."

Commit to Learning: A Classroom Toolkit

Understandably, the implications of this research may be a bit scary for teachers. It means posting a learning objective on the board will not automatically cause any learning to occur on its own. At some point, your students must decide for themselves whether to engage in learning what you've posted in front of them. Here are some brain-based steps you can take to help persuade them to commit to learning.

Give a WIIFM (What's in It for Me?)

Let's start with a simple observation: for students to commit to learning something, they must understand why they're being asked to learn it. As obvious as that sounds, it appears to be far from commonplace in many classrooms. Another Gallup survey of 5th and 11th grade students in the United States found that although 66 and 59 percent of the 5th graders, respectively, said they found "school important" and "learned something interesting" that day in school, a mere 28 and 32 percent of the 11th graders gave the same responses (Calderon, 2017). In short, the vast majority of high school students (and plenty of 5th graders) fail to see the importance of school or its relevance to them.

As it turns out, a 2006 survey of high school dropouts found that the top reason students quit school is they simply do not feel challenged or see the purpose of what they're being asked to learn (Bridgeland, DiIulio, & Morison, 2006). Most important, when asked what would keep them in school, 81 percent say providing them with real-world learning. In short, many students appear to be asking themselves what Madison Avenue advertising executives refer to as WIIFM: What's in it for me?

In light of what we know from cognitive science, it seems that many students' brains simply choose to ignore what's happening in the classroom because they deem it unworthy of their attention and energy. Although studies show that providing students with choices in learning supports their engagement and intrinsic motivation (Patall, Cooper, & Robinson, 2008), a study of several hundred elementary and middle school students found that choices alone did less to support engagement than showing students how what they're learning is important to them and connected to real life (Assor, Kaplan, & Roth, 2002). If we want students to commit to learning, we must show them how learning is relevant to them.

them—in short, what's in it for them. Here are some guiding questions that can help you show students the relevance (WIIFM) of what they're learning:

- How can I apply this knowledge or skill in my own life?
- What might I gain personally from mastering this learning?
- How might I use this new learning to help others?
- How do adults use this knowledge or skill in the real world?
- How is this knowledge or skill an important building block for my later learning?

Frame Learning as an Investigation of Big Questions

Answering big, significant questions is typically more interesting—and does more to tap into student curiosity—than answering smaller, less significant ones. Hence, an overly reductive or fragmented approach to teaching—one that loses sight of a narrative for how lessons tie together to explore a big idea or address a larger, essential question—is apt to make learning less engaging. If you haven't already, you should identify big ideas, or what Jay McTighe and Grant Wiggins (2013) call "essential questions," in what you're teaching students. Doing so helps students helps answer the WIIFM question in a more compelling way.

The key idea here is to develop open-ended questions that are not easily answered—or are, in a word, challenging. Your questions should provoke deep thought, perhaps even debate, among students. To explore them, students should have to learn and analyze new information, evaluate pros and cons, or make a personal decision based on evidence. These questions should require students to do more than simply memorize facts (though that may be a part of the process) but also think deeply about what they're learning. Here are some examples of big ideas or essential questions that can guide learning:

- For a unit on the influence of media in political life, you might ask, "How can popular opinion lead to both positive and negative changes in society?"
- For a unit on entomology, you might ask, "Which insects have the most unique 'superpowers' or special abilities humans lack?"
- For a unit on Roman history, you might ask, "In what ways was the collapse of the Roman empire, like all empires, inevitable?"
- For a unit on world history, you might ask, "How have past changes in climate exposed and accelerated political and social shifts happening in a society?"

- For a unit on argumentative writing, you might ask, "How are great writers persuasive? How do they develop arguments that inspire, captivate, and make us change our minds?"

As students grow more accustomed to experiencing lessons and units that are framed around essential questions, you may wish to encourage them to ask their own questions to experience the joy of chasing their own intellectual horizons.

Provide Learning Objectives and Success Criteria

Assuming that students now see the value of what you're asking them to learn, a new challenge emerges—one that reflects the first element of Brophy's formula for motivation: *expectancy × value*. That is, students need to believe they can actually learn what you're asking them to learn—and see what it will look like when they get there. As noted in the previous chapter, if students see their information gaps as insurmountable, they're likely to become discouraged and disengaged, so it's important to break learning into bite-sized chunks that make tackling a big idea or essential question more approachable.

Remember, too, that you want to help students take ownership of and commit to their learning. Before any of us sign on the dotted line and commit to anything, we usually like to know what exactly we're committing ourselves to doing. Similarly, your students will also be more apt to commit to learning if they know what's expected of them and why. Here's where two important strategies—learning objectives and success criteria—are essential to help students commit to learning because they define, in concrete terms, not only the purpose of their learning but also how students will make their thinking and learning visible by saying, doing, making, or writing something to demonstrate their mastery.

Learning objectives typically capture what you want your students to learn during a lesson or learning episode and why (i.e., your WIIFM). Here's a two-part formula for creating learning objectives:

We will learn ＿＿ so that [or because] ＿＿.

Following this formula consistently will help you avoid the rut many teachers fall into when it comes to learning objectives—simply restating standards without considering their importance, which ultimately tends to create busywork. For example, if you're teaching a unit on narrative writing, you might define your unit learning objective as "We will learn about effective narrative techniques so we can write an engaging anecdote for our target audience of other 10th graders."

Success criteria, on the other hand, are typically framed from students' perspectives—often as "I can" statements that help students understand and visualize what mastery will look and feel like. In so doing, success criteria help students become more active participants in their learning by understanding what's expected of them, and they help you as a teacher shift your focus from teaching to learning by clarifying not only what you'll be learning about but also what you want students to demonstrate and reflect on as they engage in learning.

In other words, learning objectives often frame your goals for teaching (e.g., "Today, we will learn about . . ."), whereas success criteria frame students' goals for learning (e.g., "I can show/explain how . . ."). Returning to the previous example ("We will learn about effective narrative techniques so we can write an engaging anecdote for our target audience of other 10th graders"), you might provide students with a series of success criteria along these lines:

- I can explain my choice of specific words to elicit emotion from my audience.
- I can use my own work as an exemplar in how to use dialogue effectively.
- I can explain the difference between metaphors and similes using an example from my own writing.
- I can use alliteration to emphasize a specific idea or feature of my narrative.

Figure 3.1 provides some additional clarification and examples.

Try This: Success Criteria Sentence Stems

These sentence stems can help you frame success criteria that encourage students to engage in deep learning.

- I can explain . . .
- I understand and can discuss . . .
- I can teach . . .
- I can defend . . .
- I can test and prove . . .
- I understand and can show . . .
- I can restate . . .

- I can use . . . to . . .
- I can discuss and explain how . . .
- I can model how to . . .
- I can demonstrate how to . . .
- I can draw a diagram that . . .
- I can choose . . .
- I can illustrate and explain . . .

Figure 3.1

Learning Objectives Versus Success Criteria

Learning Objectives	Success Criteria
What is intended learning in reference to the standards?	How will students show they have mastered the learning objective?
Why do students need to learn this? Why is it important (the WIIFM)?	How will students demonstrate they understand why they are learning this?
How do prior learning/knowledge/experiences connect to this new learning?	How will students connect this learning to prior learning and into something larger?
Examples	
We will learn about logical fallacies.	I can discuss and explain a writer's logical fallacies in a given text.
We will learn how emotions influence our decisions.	I can identify and discuss a writer's use of emotional appeals.
We will craft arguments that appeal to an audience.	I can develop an argument my target audience will want to know more about.
We will identify writers' main points.	I can teach a peer how to identify a writer's main point.

Show Students the Path to Mastery

It's also important to connect the dots between your success criteria and the driving questions around which you've framed your learning. Your success criteria should, of course, flow from these questions and add up to a larger goal for the unit. However, don't assume all students will see these connections on their own. You need to help them connect the dots—understanding how each lesson, learning objective, and success criterion adds up to or guides their learning toward the larger essential question you're exploring at the unit level.

You may find it helpful to borrow a page from television series that remind their viewers at the beginning of each episode what happened during previous episodes and end with cliff-hangers that foreshadow (or create suspense about) what will happen in the next episode. In education parlance, this is sometimes called narrative—an intentional effort to connect learning together into a bigger story, helping students see how each lesson draws them closer to a larger

learning goal. Doing so can tap into what psychologist Daniel Pink (2011) identified as one of three key drivers of intrinsic motivation—mastery—namely, seeing
ourselves advancing toward higher levels of performance. Just as it's easier to
stay committed to an exercise regimen when we see the pounds coming off when
we step on the scale, students are more apt to stay committed to learning when
they see themselves making progress.

We've seen this in classrooms, for example, at Alamanda College, a K–9
school in Melbourne, Australia, where teachers post success criteria in sequence
on the walls of their classrooms. Doing so allows students to see exactly where
they are in their learning progressions and engage in independent, self-paced,
motivated learning they can demonstrate according to visible success criteria
before moving on to the next objective in the sequence.

Encourage Personal Learning Goals

Ultimately, when students use success criteria to set and achieve their own
goals for learning, the real magic happens in a classroom. When we achieve
goals we've set for ourselves, our brains fill with the same chemical (dopamine)
as when we eat chocolate, finish grading a stack of papers, or win a prize at the
county fair. In short, achieving goals feels good and forms a positive addiction.
Of course, goals are more meaningful when we set them for ourselves rather
than having them handed to us. What we're talking about here is really just common sense; few of us would appreciate someone telling us what our New Year's
resolution ought to be, yet that's more or less what we do when we give learning
goals to students and don't invite their buy-in.

By the same token, learning goals should also be challenging; 25 years of
research shows stretch goals encourage greater effort and persistence than
wishy-washy "do your best" goals or no goals (Locke & Latham, 2006). Stretch
goals, almost by definition, are designed to set students up for a bit of 4. That's
OK, so long as students view their failures with the right mindset.

As it turns out, students who adopt performance goals, which tend to be
about wanting to look smart and avoid looking dumb (e.g., "I want an *A* in my
English class"), tend to feel helpless, inadequate, and crestfallen when the going
gets tough. However, students who adopt so-called learning goals, which reflect "a
desire to learn new skills, master new tasks, or understand new things—a desire
to get smarter" (e.g., "I want to become a better writer"), are more apt to take initial failures in stride and press on to accomplish their goals (Dweck, 2000, p. 15).

Certainly, some students are highly motivated by grades. They may even ask you directly, "What do I need to do to get an *A*?" However, simply getting a good grade is a performance goal, which can lead to fixed mindsets and frustration. Besides, it's a rather meager way to approach learning. Ideally, you'll help all students set personal learning goals. One way to help students develop their own learning goals is to ask them to start with the big idea or essential question for a unit and then write their own "I can" statements or use a K-W-L chart to identify what they *know*, what they *wonder*, and then what they've *learned*, like this:

- What do I know? (e.g., "Mars is a rocky planet, and it has ice, an atmosphere, and seasons")
- What do I wonder? (e.g., "Can human beings ever live on Mars?")
- What have I learned? (e.g., "I learned about terraforming and the possibility of water beneath Martian soil").

With facilitation, a K-W-L chart can help students turn what they wonder about or want to learn into a personal learning goal (e.g., "I want to be able to explain why some people say humans will live on Mars by the end of the century, why others say it's impossible, and what I think is possible or impossible").

Help Students Commit to Effort

Setting goals is important, but as it turns out, many students often don't know how to translate their aspirations into achievement—as Harvard researcher Roland Fryer Jr. (2013) discovered when he offered 18,000 students in four cities a total of $6.3 million in rewards to improve their academic performance but found no effects for the intervention. Why? Basically, students *were* motivated by the promise of rewards but had no idea how to do better. "Not a single student," wrote Fryer, mentioned "reading the textbook, studying harder, completing their homework, or asking teachers . . . about confusing topics" (p. 33).

Therefore, it's important to teach students—often quite directly—the link between effort and achieving their goals. Psychologist Martin Seligman (1990), who has dedicated his career to identifying what makes some people more successful than others, has found that successful people chalk up their own successes (and failures) to their efforts (or lack thereof) versus luck or misfortune—a phenomenon he called "learned optimism" versus learned helplessness. Learned optimism, Seligman noted, can be developed through mastery experiences—or opportunities to experience success, even at a small scale. Over time, small-scale successes begin to show students that their own success isn't simply the result of chance, a teacher liking them, or their innate ability but of their own efforts. Conversely, if they're unable to link success or failure to their own efforts, they are more apt to develop learned helplessness.

This single factor, sometimes called fate control, has been found to have a more powerful positive (or negative) influence on student achievement than any other factor within a school's control (Coleman, 1966). Over the past few decades, in fact, researchers have found that where students' perceptions fall along a continuum of locus of control—from internal (believing they can shape their life outcomes through their own actions) to external (seeing their circumstances as shaped by forces beyond their control)—is one of the strongest predictors of success in school and life. For example, high school dropouts are more apt to have an external locus of control (Ekstrom, Goertz, Pollack, & Rock, 1986), whereas high-achieving low-income minority students are more likely to have an internal locus of control (Finn & Rock, 1997).

In fact, for minority students, a strong internal locus of control can counteract the detrimental effects of stereotype threat—a well-documented phenomenon of students performing poorly when they feel at risk of being judged on the basis of their race, gender, or other social identity. For example, a meta-analysis (Richardson, Abraham, & Bond, 2012) found that feeling in control over one's life combined with academic self-efficacy and goal orientation accounted for roughly 20 percent of the variance in university students' grade point averages—nearly the same predictive power as high school grade point average and college entrance exam scores.

What may be most striking (and worrisome), however, is that an analysis of thousands of surveys of college students over the past 40 years has found that, on average, students' locus of control has become more external: the average college student in 2002 had a more external locus of control than 80 percent of college students in the early 1960s (Twenge, Zhang, & Im, 2004). The researchers who studied this phenomenon speculate that shifts in our cultural ethos may be to blame as our society has moved from a prevailing belief that hard work is the ticket to a better life toward a view that individuals are powerless in the face of uncaring institutions, unpredictable outside forces, or uncontrollable elements of one's own mental makeup (e.g., being diagnosed with ADHD).

The good news here is that providing students with small opportunities to set and achieve goals can reverse these effects by helping them link effort to their own success, which in turn begets a more internal locus of control. Bandura and Schunk (1981), for example, found that providing students with short-term achievable or "proximal" personal learning goals (e.g., aiming to complete six pages of instructional items during each class session) helped them achieve at higher levels than students who set "distal" learning goals (e.g., aspiring to complete all 42 pages over 7 sessions) or who set no goals at all. Moreover, accomplishing these small goals also appeared to help students foster the first kernels of an internal locus of control—a greater belief in their ability to overcome challenges with effort.

The Big Idea: Connecting *What* with *Why* to Encourage Commitment to Learning

The key takeaway in all of this research and guidance is that for our students to commit to learning, they must tell themselves these two things: (1) *This is interesting and important*, and (2) *I believe I can learn/master it*. In sum, the most important thing you may ever share with a student isn't learning itself but, rather, the determination to commit to learning.

Before embarking on any learning journey with students, it's important to spend time helping them understand not only what they will learn but also why they should learn it—that is, their WIIFM. In hindsight, had I done that with *The Scarlet Letter*, I might have helped my students see that digging into its dense prose would not only help them sharpen their close reading skills but also unearth deep truths of human existence, such as the tension between social mores and personal freedom, which is as relevant for us today as it was for Hawthorne and the Puritans he wrote about.

At the same time, it's equally important to help students see the path to mastery—how achieving a series of small wins (i.e., their success criteria) will add to something larger and more valuable, such as achieving a personal goal for learning. In so doing, you can help students develop what may be the most important gift we can give them—an internal locus of control or sense of learned optimism.

At the end of the novel, when Hester Prynne finally loses her scarlet letter, Hawthorne writes, "She had not known the weight until she felt the freedom." So, too, it may be for our students. When we help them find purpose and meaning in what they're learning and a belief that through effort they can achieve their goals, we can unburden them of the strain of trying to learn something they find meaningless as well as pernicious self-doubt about themselves as learners.

4

Focus on New Learning

We've likely all had the embarrassing experience of meeting someone for the first time at a social gathering and realizing a minute or two into the conversation that, despite having told us their name when we first met, we've completely forgotten it. Was it Shannon or Sarah? Brad or Brett? Admittedly, this has happened often enough to me that my wife knows the desperate look on my face when I call her over to introduce herself so they will repeat their names. (*Oh, yes, Sally and Barry—that's right.*)

What's going on inside our brains when this happens reflects a core principle of learning—namely, that we remember what we think about. Once we hear someone's name—unless it strikes us as unusual or notable—most of us stop thinking about it; we proceed to talk with our new acquaintance about other things and, regrettably, fail to remember the person's name. Some memory experts say that to remember a name, we've got to say it aloud a few times immediately after learning it ("Great to meet you, Sally. Where do you work, Barry?") and immediately associate it with something memorable (and often visual) about the person: Smiling Sally, Balding Barry (said silently, of course).

In short, we've got to focus on what we've just learned to transfer what's in our immediate memory into our working memory. Typically, we do this by actively thinking about the information and combining it with other sensory inputs (e.g., the sound of the person's name or a visual cue as you say it aloud). Doing so causes more of our neurons to fire their memory codes, connecting with other neurons, and in so doing, creating a richer and stronger memory.

All of this demonstrates the incredible power—and frustrating shortcomings—of our working memory, which we'll explore in this chapter. By this point in our model, we have helped students become interested in learning and then helped them commit to learning. You might think of the first two stages of the learning model as akin to the old story about the veteran salesperson who reminds his younger counterpart that his job isn't to lead people to water but to make them thirsty. So, as you've engaged your students in the first two phases of the learning model, they have hopefully become thirsty for new learning.

But we're not done. We need to help students hold that information in their working memory, which requires a number of mental processes, not the least of which is actively thinking about their learning. Basically, at this point, the challenge shifts to ensuring they remain focused on new learning so they can hold the new information, like Sally's and Barry's names, in their working memories long enough to recall it later.

As you'll see in this chapter, there are many ways to do this, including engaging students in question-and-answer sessions, closely reading a text, following a process as it's modeled, creating a nonlinguistic representation (e.g., drawing a picture) of new concepts, or taking notes during a lecture. All these active learning processes, especially when used in combination, help knowledge soak deeper into the brain.

Too often at this point, though, teachers fall back on orchestrating lessons around what they're doing as teachers rather than what needs to happen in students' minds. That is, instead of thinking about what we want our students to be thinking about, we often revert back to "presenting" a lesson and filling in problems 1–10.

With that in mind, how do we ensure what's happening in the classroom doesn't simply go in one ear and out the other? We'll begin our exploration of this question by digging deeper into what we know about one of the more perplexing and fickle components of our information processing system: working memory.

The Science of Focused Attention

Our short-term working memory basically consists of our conscious thoughts, such as the names of the couple we've just met at a cocktail party. Cognitive science suggests we can hold information in our working memory for anywhere from 5 to 20 minutes before it either decays—a victim of our brain's ongoing efforts to prune information it deems useless—or continues the journey to long-term memory. Like all learning, holding information in our working memory takes an effort that our brains prefer to put toward other mental activities.

Generally speaking, our conscious thoughts tend to be verbal (the commentary in our brains, sometimes called our stream of consciousness), visual, and spatial. Research from Baddeley and Hitch (1974) identifies three key systems: a phonological loop (which deals with written or spoken words), a visuospatial sketchpad (which handles visual images and navigation), and a central executive system that coordinates the first two systems. Baddeley and Logie (1999) later added a fourth system, the episodic buffer, which is something of a warehouse manager for prior knowledge (e.g., going to the "storeroom," so to speak).

Imagine, for example, you're driving to a relative's home in an unfamiliar town. According to this model, your phonological loop will help you read street signs and listen to directions on your phone, your visuospatial sketchpad will help you navigate your vehicle, the central executive system will direct these other two systems to stay alert, and your episodic buffer may recall landmarks your relative said were important to avoid missing the turn off the main road. With all of this going on in your working memory, you may be apt turn down your radio and shush the kids in the back seat to help you concentrate.

Although this model remains theoretical (e.g., scientists have yet to "find" the visuospatial sketchpad in the brain), it is a model that is nonetheless based on scientific theory—including observations from numerous experiments that have found we're able to handle streams of verbal and visual information simultaneously but not two streams of verbal information or visuospatial information at the same time.

You've likely experienced this yourself. For example, you probably have no trouble processing visual and verbal streams of information at the same time—like reading words on an image or listening to the radio while you're driving your car. However, you're likely to have difficulty simultaneously processing more than one stream of the same kind of information—for example, reading when someone is sitting next to you talking on the phone or trying to rub your belly and pat your head at the same time.

Of course, as we automate mental functions, our working memories can engage in increasingly complex activities without directing as much mental bandwidth to them. For example, you can read individual words in a sentence without sounding out each individual letter, listen to someone speak in your native tongue without focusing on every word they're saying, or type an e-mail without considering where each letter is on the keyboard. These automated scripts notwithstanding, studies show that processing written words still requires most of us to engage in an additional step of mental processing—namely, translating written words into verbal ones in our brains, which explains why reading a passage of text often feels more effortful than listening to a presentation.

Unless, of course, we're experiencing death by PowerPoint—the dreadful (yet all too common) practice of enduring someone reading words off a screen to us, which are often the same words on the handout in front of us. One reason such presentations are so unbearable is that they push our phonological loop to the brink and require us to process words in triplicate—orally and written, twice—on the slide and the handout (Medina, 2008).

We might think of it this way: our phonological loop and visuospatial sketchpad operate like two separate channels into the brain; they can operate simultaneously but tend to clog up if we cram too much information into either of them at once. As it turns out, this core principle of working memory points to some important ways we can make learning easier, more effective, and more engaging for students.

Pairing Graphics with Words

Given these two channels in our working memories, it's not surprising that studies have found pairing graphics with words to be one of the most effective strategies available to support learning (Greenberg et al., 2016; Mayer, 2011). Basically, our visual and verbal systems are most effective when triggered together. When we receive information orally, we only retain 10 percent of it three days later, but when a powerful image accompanies it, we recall 65 percent of it three days later (Medina, 2008). A McREL meta-analysis of research on effective teaching strategies found, in fact, that supporting new learning with nonlinguistic representations, such as graphic organizers, is one of the most effective teaching strategies (Beesley & Apthorp, 2010).

Illustrating Abstract Ideas with Concrete Examples

This same principle—simultaneously triggering the visual and verbal systems—is likely at work with another strategy that studies have shown helps students assimilate new information: illustrating abstract concepts with concrete examples (Mayer, 2011; Paivio, 1971; Weinstein, Madan, & Sumerack, 2018). Scientists have long observed that we are more apt to recall concrete nouns than abstract ones—for example, *button* is more memorable than *bound* (Gorman, 1961). Similarly, we're better able to recall abstract concepts when we can visualize them (Paivio, 1971).

As it turns out, numerous classroom experiments support providing students with both abstract concepts and concrete examples (Pashler, Rohrer, Cepeda, & Carpenter, 2007). This makes sense when we consider the dual channels of our working memory. We can make better sense of abstract ideas (articulated verbally) when they are illustrated with concrete examples (provided visually). Conversely, we often don't see the underlying pattern or principle within concrete examples unless someone makes it explicit (i.e., verbalizes it) for us.

For example, to understand the abstract concept of a food chain, we need both an abstract definition (e.g., "a hierarchical series of organisms each dependent on the next as a source of food") as well as concrete examples we can visualize (e.g., insects ⇨ birds ⇨ bobcats). Illustrating abstract ideas with concrete examples thus appears to support dual encoding—helping students' brains assimilate new information both verbally and visually.

Weaving Together Problem Solving with Worked Examples

Numerous studies have also shown that in mathematics and science classrooms, in particular, students better acquire new learning when they have opportunities to shift back and forth between attempting to solve problems on their own and seeing examples of worked solutions (Pashler et al., 2007). For example, in one experiment (Sweller & Cooper, 1985), students were given eight algebra problems. For the experimental group, half of the problems were already solved; for the control group, all eight problems were unsolved. Afterward, students in the experimental group who bounced back and forth between worked examples and new problems to solve performed significantly better on a posttest. Similar benefits have also been found in studies with younger students (Zhu & Simon, 1987).

In short, combining productive struggle with provided answers appears to accelerate student learning, likely because it requires students to internalize dual coding and think through problems (i.e., engage in internal verbalizing) as they tackle them (e.g., "Let's see—I think need to find the lowest common denominator first") while double-checking their thinking with provided answers (e.g., a visual example of how to find the lowest common denominator). As it turns out, such self-talk has been shown to be critical in assimilating new learning, which brings us to the next key principle for helping students focus on new learning.

Asking Questions as We're Learning

Self-questioning—that is, cultivating a voice in our heads that assesses where we are with our learning—has been shown to be a powerful strategy for supporting learning. When properly cultivated, our inner voice sustains our curiosity and guides our learning by saying things like, "Wait, I don't get this." For example, if we're watching a science show and hear that starlight in the night sky emanates from stars that may no longer exist, a voice in our heads may say, "Wait, I don't get that," as we grab the remote to rewind the program. These kinds of questions can also help us connect what we're learning with our prior knowledge—the process at the heart of all learning. "Oh, right," we tell ourselves. "Starlight travels at the speed of light." Self-questions can also help us identify abstract ideas from concrete examples: The universe is unfathomably large and ever-expanding. This inner voice can also lead to other questions to further guide our learning: "How exactly do astronomers measure the distance of far-away stars, anyway?"

As it turns out, providing even relatively brief training to enhance the central executive of our working memory—teaching it to ask these sorts of questions while we're learning—has been shown to have powerful effects on comprehension of not just reading but also oral lectures. One study that trained 9th graders to ask themselves compare-and-contrast, causal-relationship questions; analysis questions; and self-reflection questions while listening to history lectures found these techniques had significant effects on student learning. How much? It was the equivalent of a full letter grade or more on subsequent tests of knowledge (King, 1991). Though the sample size of this initial study was small, its findings have since been replicated with other groups of students, including high school vocational students (Pate & Miller, 2011) and 4th and 5th graders with learning disabilities (Wanzek, Wexler, Vaughn, & Ciullo, 2010).

Indeed, of the seven strategies called out by the National Reading Panel in its review of hundreds of studies on reading comprehension, two reflected student self-questioning—namely, "comprehension monitoring, where readers learn how to be aware of their understanding of the material" and "question generation, where readers ask themselves questions about the various aspects of the story" (National Institute of Child Health and Human Development, 2000, p. 15). What may perhaps be most striking in these studies is the limited training time (about 90 minutes total) required to produce large and lasting improvements in student performance—likely by heightening the ability of students' central executive system in their working memories to keep their visual and verbal systems focused on learning.

Taking Notes (by Hand)

A McREL synthesis of numerous studies of effective instructional practices (Beesley & Apthorp, 2010) found that taking notes while learning had a significant effect size (.90) on learning. Experimental studies have found students who were encouraged to take notes during a college lecture demonstrated greater learning than both a second comparison group that took no notes and instead wrote an essay afterward about what they'd learned and a third comparison group that was told to simply review the content of the lecture afterward (Beeson, 1996).

All of this goes to show that students are more likely to remember stuff when they take notes on it. However, taking notes by typing them onto a laptop or tablet appears to erase these benefits. Students often type faster than they can write and thus more easily take copious notes, yet doing so doesn't actually result in greater learning, likely because note taking isn't supposed to be easy or a transcription of what's said in a classroom.

What's more important is actively engaging in learning by considering the key ideas of new learning, summarizing it in our own words, and writing it down. A Princeton University study (Mueller & Oppenheimer, 2014) found that while laptop users wrote more words while taking notes, more wasn't better. At issue seems to be something cognitive scientist Daniel Willingham (2003) has noted—namely, that "students remember . . . what they think about." For students who are efficient typists, laptops may make it easy to mindlessly record what they hear, instead of thinking about what they're learning—mentally connecting dots and focusing on what's most important.

On top of that, the very act of handwriting appears to have some important cognitive benefits. Neuroscience studies have shown that compared to typing, writing by hand activates more regions of the brain—in particular, visual processing centers at the heart of perceiving letters (James & Engelhardt, 2012). In sum, note taking appears to be an effective learning aid because it prompts students to invest effort in thinking about their learning, which writing by hand fosters better because it supports dual processing—turning the verbal learning of spoken words into visual learning of notes on a page.

Basically, note taking *should* be a mental chore that demands more effort, or what cognitive scientists Robert and Elizabeth Bjork (1992) dubbed "desirable difficulties." Studies have found, for example, that adding small speed bumps to learning slows down learning but increases comprehension and recall. The act of generation during learning (including writing down what's important in a lecture) creates such a speed bump; it requires multiple parts of our brains to engage with what we're learning, which is why we're more apt to learn and remember what we write down. In short, what matters more when taking notes isn't the notes themselves, but rather the act of taking them.

Focus on New Learning: A Classroom Toolkit

These principles of working memory point to several evidence-based instructional strategies, many of which are likely already in your repertoire. With a deeper understanding of students' working memories, though, you'll be able to apply these strategies with greater intentionality, seeing more clearly when and where to integrate them into learning opportunities. As you do that, you'll likely find that your toolkit of strategies is now even more powerful.

Use Nonlinguistic Representations

As we've seen, our brains process information more effectively when images and physical sensations (i.e., nonlinguistic representations) accompany spoken or written words. These representations can be in the form of pictures, drawings, and models along with smells, sounds, tastes, and physical touch and movement (Dean et al., 2012), all of which help students integrate linguistic knowledge with mental images of what they're learning.

Here are some specific strategies you can use to support your students' visual learning in the classroom:

- Use "mind maps" that encourage students to draw diagrams that show the interrelationships between ideas (e.g., the elements of the Renaissance, photosynthesis, or irregular verbs in English) to help them see important connections between ideas or create working mental models of complex processes.
- Create physical models or use manipulatives (e.g., blocks to aid in counting, 3D topographical maps, sentence diagrams) to help them grasp abstract concepts with more concrete representations.

- Encourage students to develop mental pictures of what they're learning (e.g., "Imagine what it would've been like for a medieval mariner to navigate out of sight of land, surrounded by the ocean, with nothing but the stars to guide you") to help them better comprehend challenging material.
- Ask students to draw pictures, illustrations, and symbols of what they're learning (e.g., "In your notes, create icons that represent autocracy, oligarchy, and representative and direct democracy") to help them distinguish key differences among related concepts.
- Engage in kinesthetic activities (e.g., going out to the schoolyard and arranging students to represent the solar system at scale) to help them understand and appreciate otherwise unfathomable facts and concepts.

Show and Tell

As noted earlier, it's important to illustrate complex ideas with concrete examples and, conversely, to make explicit the underlying principles, abstract ideas, and big ideas reflected in concrete examples. Basically, you need to *tell* students the abstract idea and then *show* them what it looks like—or vice versa: show students concrete examples and then tell them the principle they illustrate. Figure 4.1 provides some examples of what this might look like in classrooms.

Figure 4.1
Connecting Abstract Ideas with Concrete Examples

Abstract Idea	Concrete Examples
Supply and Demand: the idea that as unit prices rise, demand decreases and vice versa	• A pizza parlor sells 100 pizzas per night for $15 apiece. When it raises its prices to $20, it only sells 50 pizzas. • A vendor selling hot dogs drops its price from $5 to $4 and finds its sales increase 30 percent.
Antihero: a lead character who has good intentions but many flaws, often lacking the traits of traditional heroes	• George Milton, *Of Mice and Men* • Daisy Buchanan, *The Great Gatsby* • Lady Macbeth, *Macbeth* • Walter Lee Younger, *A Raisin in the Sun*
Quadratic Equation: an equation with at least one term squared; graphs of a quadratic equation form parabolas	• $ax^2 + bx + c = 0$ • A ball is thrown straight up in the air from 1 m above the ground at a velocity of 14 m/s. How high will it go, and when will it hit the ground? Assuming gravity pulls on the ball at 5 m/s, we solve for h (height) with this equation: $h = 1 + 14t + 5t^2$.

Try This: Concreteness Fading

This method, supported by research, begins with the teacher sharing concrete examples (often three), and then gradually replacing them with abstract representations (Fyfe, McNeil, Son, & Goldstone, 2014). For example, in a math class, you might demonstrate subtraction first with manipulatives, then represent the manipulatives as squares, and finally replace them with numbers and mathematical operands. In science, you might begin with a concrete example of ants foraging for food, then represent the ants as black dots and food as green triangles to illustrate an abstract idea like competitive specialization.

Although it seems natural to start with an abstract concept and subsequently illustrate it with concrete examples, you may find it more effective to start with concrete examples from which you extract the abstract idea—an approach reflected in the "concreteness fading" method described in the sidebar.

Model Steps to Mastery with Direct Instruction

One of the most effective strategies for helping students focus on new learning, especially with procedural (skills-based) learning, is to show them the process one step at a time. When helping students develop a skill—such as "carrying the one" with multidigit addition, editing prose for conciseness, engaging in close reading, or balancing chemical equations—it's often best to first show students the steps you want them to learn so they see what mastery learning looks like. This is sometimes called the "I do" phase—you model for students what a process looks like in practice with straightforward, direct instruction. Doing so helps support dual (verbal and visual) processing of new learning.

For example, instead of simply providing verbal directions (e.g., "As you edit your essays, convert passive voice to active voice"), show students how to engage in the process and provide them with your own thinking aloud as you do it (e.g., "So when I see a phrase like 'It is widely believed,' I say, 'Oops, that's passive voice because the subject of the sentence, *it*, isn't actually doing the action but rather receiving it—the people who are believing 'it' are the ones doing the action. So I'm going to rewrite the sentence to make it read more like how our brains work: 'People widely believe that . . . .' Do you see how that's easier for your brain to follow what we're trying to say here?"). After demonstrating a process a few times, you can invite students to follow along as you engage in the process together (e.g., the "we do" phase described in the following section).

Alternate Worked Problems with Problems Students Must Solve

As noted earlier, weaving together problem solving with worked examples has been shown to accelerate assimilation of new learning. One way to do this is to invite students to engage in a process they're learning with you—for example, following the same steps for multidigit addition—in their own workbooks as you walk them through the steps. This is sometimes referred to as the "we do" phase. Students may also do this independently if you give them opportunities to alternate between solved problems (along the process for solving them) and problems to solve on their own.

Research suggests that this approach is most effective when the provided solutions gradually fade away, requiring students to increasingly work the problems independently (e.g., Renkl, Atkinson, & Große, 2004). Also, studies have found that worked examples are most effective when they integrate text and visual guidance—for example, providing students with an animated video that shows them how to work through a problem.

Although it may be easiest to picture alternating worked and unsolved problems in math or science classrooms (which is, incidentally, where these studies mostly occurred), this strategy also works in other subjects. I discovered this myself as a graduate student, when fresh out of college, I found myself teaching composition to first-year college students (and donning a necktie in a futile effort to look older than my students). Our graduate coordinator cleverly required all of the instructors to write the same essays we assigned to our students. His rationale was simple: don't ask students to do something you can't do yourself.

Writing the essays myself not only reminded me of the skills each form of writing (narrative, persuasive, expository, etc.) required but also gave me a model (i.e., a worked example) to share with my students—one that I could walk them through to explain the choices I made as a writer and show them how I worked and reworked my thesis statement, used details to support an argument, and edited for conciseness and clarity. That's what they most wanted to see—how to take bad writing and make it better. Therefore, I started to create examples of "unsolved" problems—unedited, turgid, passive-voice-laden prose.

First, I'd model how to hack away at it, creating a "worked" example (an "I do" process). Then we'd edit a few sentences together as a class ("we do") before I'd let them tackle some sentences on their own ("you do").

Teach Self-Questioning and Close Reading

You'll recall from the previous section that studies have found teaching students to quiz themselves while learning boosts both comprehension and retention. One such approach, called TWA (**think** before reading, think **while** reading, think **after** reading), has been shown to have a tremendous effect size (.99) on students' abilities to assess main ideas, summarize, and retell narratives (Mason, Snyder, Sukhram, & Kedem, 2006). Here's a simple set of questions, drawn from research, that you can teach students to ask themselves anytime they engage in learning new material:

- What's the main point?
- What's an example of this?
- How is this similar to/different from what I already know?
- Could I explain how it works/why it's true to someone else?
- How might I use this?
- What do I think about it?
- What do I still not understand?

To be sure, many students already ask themselves these sorts of questions as they assimilate new information. In fact, it's this ability to self-evaluate that often distinguishes more successful learners from those who struggle. That said, we shouldn't assume students know how to employ this strategy; moreover, you may need to model it by showing them how to pause occasionally during reading to ask themselves one of these questions or how to engage in active listening (and self-questioning) during a lecture.

In Chapter 6, we'll return to this idea—the power of quizzing oneself while engaging in relearning—as we dive more deeply into the practice and reflect phase of learning and, in particular, show how students can often study less yet learn more simply by asking themselves questions about what they've learned. Nonetheless, during this phase in the learning model—focus on new learning—self-questions are powerful because they help students keep their brains engaged in active learning while in class or reading.

Engage Students in Active Note Taking

Here are a few strategies you can use in your classroom to help students engage in active note taking:

- **Teach students how to take notes.** Specifically, model for students what they ought to include in their notes. For example, as you're explaining a concept or procedure, pause for a moment to show students (using a projector if you have one) what you'd write down in your notes if you were a student. Here, you can show students how notes capture key ideas, rather than record verbatim everything that's being said. You can also show how to use bulleted lists to capture key ideas, create drawings and graphics to help them later visualize the learning, use lines to connect concepts, and circle or underline key words they want to remember later.

- **Focus student note taking with guided notes.** One of the more effective ways to keep students focused on and thinking about their learning—and learn how to take notes—is to provide them with fill-in-the-blank outlines or partially completed notes as they listen to a lecture, read a text, or watch a video. A meta-analysis of this technique (known as guided notes) found they supported significant gains in learning, especially over the loosely structured approach in which students are simply encouraged to take notes (Larwin, Dawson, Erickson, & Larwin, 2012). While it might seem gimmicky, guided notes work because they help students see what's important and support their engagement because each incomplete blank creates a knowledge gap (or dose of curiosity) for students. They have, in fact, been found to be effective with a wide range of students, including those with disabilities and those in college.

- **Encourage students to draw pictures of key concepts.** Studies show drawing pictures of words helps us better recall those words than a variety of other techniques, including rewriting notes, visualizing learning, or passively looking at images (Wammes, Meade, & Fernandes, 2016). You can apply this in a classroom setting by encouraging students to draw pictures or icons of important concepts and vocabulary terms, like electrons, oligarchy, and parabolas.

- **Ask students to take notes by hand.** As noted earlier, research is pretty clear on this one: taking notes by typing them on a laptop is far less effective than old-fashioned handwritten notes. You can explain this research to students, then ask them to close their laptops and get out their trusty pencils and notebooks.

Try This: Guided Notes

Here are three formats you can use to guide student note taking (Silver, Abla, Boutz, & Perini, 2018):

- **Window notes.** Students divide pages into quadrants labeled "facts," "feelings and reactions," "questions," and "connections." While reading, listening to a lecture, engaging in a class discussion, or watching a video, they fill in each quadrant.
- **Split screen notes.** Students divide pages into two columns, one labeled "Sketch" and the other "Big Ideas and Important Details," and create rows based on the number of "chunks" or segments you want to cover in a lesson. Students sketch each concept and record big ideas and details in their notes.
- **Webbing.** Students begin with a key question or concept in the center of a page and then draw supporting concepts and details "branching off" the main idea in a web to create a graphic organizer of their learning.

The Big Idea: We Learn What We Put into Pictures, Words, and Thoughts

Basically, all of this research and guidance can be boiled down to this key takeaway: [if we want students to assimilate and encode new learning—that is, focus on new learning—we must help them see what they're learning, put it into their own words, and think about what they're learning.]

Let's dispel a myth here: there is no such thing as a visual learner, because practically everyone is a visual learner. So, as you design learning opportunities for students, it's important to consider how you'll help them visualize what they're learning, providing them with graphics, images, and other nonlinguistic representations, showing them the steps in a process and worked solutions, and sharing concrete examples that illustrate abstract ideas.

At the same time, though, because we assimilate new information into our brains via our visuospatial sketchpad and phonological loop, it's important to provide the running commentary in our heads (the phonological loop) with words on which to hang new concepts. Thus, we need to help students verbalize their learning by designing learning opportunities that encourage them to put what they're experiencing into their own words. Here, self-questions and translating what they're learning into words on a page supports assimilation of new information.

Finally, it's important to recall this simple principle from cognitive scientist Daniel Willingham: we only learn what we think about. Thus, as students assimilate and encode new information, we need to ensure they're actively thinking about (and, we might add, staying curious about) what they're learning—not simply going along for the ride as passive participants in the classroom. We'll dig more deeply into this idea in the next chapter on helping students make sense of learning, where we'll explore what it takes to help students engage in another fundamental learning process: connecting new learning with prior learning and consolidating disparate bits of information into cohesive mental models.

5

Make Sense of Learning

You may recall the late '80s and early '90s TV series *MacGyver* in which the eponymous mullet-wearing star of the show would improvise solutions for getting out of jams (usually as a time bomb ticked away) with readily available objects—for example, rigging a machine gun out of a cord, string, stick, and matches. At this point in the learning process, your students now face a MacGyver-like challenge: They've become interested in, committed to, and focused on new learning. Now, they must make sensible, workable connections among disparate bits of information before their working memories become fatigued and "time out."

Basically, the peril new learning faces at the point is ensuring our brains don't turn into the *Saturday Night Live* parody of MacGyver: the bumbling Mac-Gruber, an action hero prone to distractions who ended nearly every sketch by turning away from the ticking bomb to offer platitudinous soliloquies as it exploded. If our brains become distracted or are forced to juggle too many things at once, our learning may come to an unseemly (though less violent) end as our brains discard information it deems useless. In this chapter, we'll explore how our working memories encode new information (and the perils information faces during this phase), so you can help your students engage in this next key phase of the learning process: make sense of learning.

The Science of Comprehension

We've probably all had the experience of something not making sense. Maybe staring at charts in an Econ 101 class in college. A doctor explaining a diagnosis. Trying to understand the rules of a new card game. We hear the words. We see the pictures. Yet can't string them together into anything that resembles a coherent picture.

You've probably also heard students saying something similar, despite your best efforts to provide them with new learning. You've explained things thoroughly, worked through problems, provided graphics, and shown concrete examples, yet they still say, "This doesn't make sense." When you hear this, what are students really telling you?

The answer has a lot to do with how our brains work, starting with a process that's not yet fully understood by cognitive scientists: encoding. Basically, as our brains take in new information, we begin to make visual and verbal representations of that image in our brain that we can return to later, called memory traces (Brown, Roediger, & McDaniel, 2014).

The Mystery of Encoding

Exactly how all of this happens remains a bit of a mystery. "The little we do know suggests it is like a blender left running with the lid off," writes cognitive scientist John Medina. "The information is literally sliced into discrete pieces as it enters the brain and is splattered all over the insides of our mind" (2008, p. 104). For example, brain scans show that when our brains see complex pictures, they store diagonal and vertical lines in different regions. Scientists have also caught glimpses of the mysterious ways our brains encode information from stroke survivors; for example, one woman who had a stroke in a tiny part of her brain could still write in complete sentences yet dropped out all the vowels, which suggests her brain stored consonants in a different place than vowels.

Through a process that's not yet fully understood, our brains seamlessly reconstruct these "blenderized" bits of data back into a sensible representation of what we've learned and observed. Basically, as sensory data enter our brains, our brains translate them into stored electrical impulses that, when reactivated, re-create the original impulses in our minds—a memory. Scientists call the process of converting one form of electrical impulse (sensory input) into a new set of electrical patterns (memories) that our brains later reproduce encoding (Medina, 2008).

Sometimes, our brains do this automatically, especially when new information is fused with strong emotions. We don't need a highlighter pen or flash cards to remember special or tragic moments in our lives—such as a marriage proposal or a car accident. Our brains simply spring to action and embed them straight into our memories. At other times, though, we must help our brains gather those pieces of learning that have been splattered around in what is called effortful processing (Medina, 2008), which lies at the heart of most academic learning.

Cracking the Encoding Code

When it comes to verbal learning, cognitive scientists believe our brains encode (i.e., engage in effortful processing of) new learning in these three ways (Medina, 2008):

- Semantic encoding: processing the meaning of words.
- Phonemic encoding: processing the sound of words.
- Structural encoding: processing what words look like.

Why does this matter? As it turns out, how we encode information influences how well we recall that information later. For example, when researchers gave two groups of participants a list of words and asked one group to identify the number of words with diagonal lines in the letters and the second group to consider the meaning of each word as well as rate how much they like or dislike it on a scale from 1 to 10, the second group recalled two to three times as many words as the first group (Medina, 2008). Basically, the first group engaged in more superficial encoding of the words, whereas the second group considered the meaning of each word and rated it, adding another association it. What this suggests, according to Medina, is that "we remember things much better the more elaborately we encode what we encounter, especially if we can personalize it" (p. 111).

Cognitive scientist Daniel Willingham (2003) puts it even more succinctly: we "remember what we think about." That is, if we are to learn anything, we must concentrate on visual and verbal inputs as they enter our brains; connect them to memories, other ideas, images, and emotions; and help us make sense of them to create meaning. Although we're not exactly sure how this happens, we can nonetheless extract some key principles and big ideas from cognitive science that we can, in turn, apply to help students encode learning for later use by first making sense of what they're learning.

Messy Neural Networks

Here's big idea number 1: We don't store memories in our brains like papers in a filing cabinet, neatly arranging bits of data into tidy mental folders. Rather, we appear to store them by connecting memories, ideas, and experiences together into messy neural networks. That's why we tend to associate words together, and the recollection of one memory often leads us to recall another. It also means that to learn anything, we must connect it to prior knowledge. As we've seen, the more connections we can make to new learning, the more likely we will be to recall the information later.

The same is true for skills-based learning. A new skill tends to feel clumsy or mechanistic until we connect it to other processes that form an automated script in our minds. For example, when learning to drive a car, a driver-in-training must consciously concentrate on several distinct steps: activate the turn signal, turn the wheel, let off the gas and apply the brake, avoid the curb, and ignore the passenger nervously clutching the dashboard. For more experienced drivers, those actions get consolidated into a single, automated script: turn right.

7 (or Maybe 4) Is the Magic Number

Here's the second big idea: Our working memories have bandwidth limitations. We can only MacGyver together a limited number of disparate bits of information before we run into trouble. As we covered in Chapter 1, this limit averages at seven or even maybe as few as four.

You've likely experienced this yourself. Consider, for example, if your significant other or housemate calls you at work and asks you to pick up coffee, milk, trash bags, and bagels from the store on your way home. You're likely to simplify the list and repeat it back (mentally or verbally)—*coffee, milk, bags,* and *bagels*—and think, "OK, got it." However, if they call you back a few minutes later and say, "Oh, wait. We also need eggplant, dog food, chicken, asparagus, and lettuce," now you have a problem. You might, perhaps, try a mnemonic trick: turning the shopping list into an acronym you can hold in your memory until you check out at the store: CMB-BED-CAL, which you might turn into a three-word phrase—CoMB, BED, CAL—and picture a *comb,* lying on your *bed,* next to your bed stand where you put your phone to make a *call.*

Or you might just say, "Umm . . . how about you text me that list?"

All of this illustrates how our working memories operate—by clustering disparate bits of information into larger, more meaningful patterns. A key implication of this is that if we introduce too much information to students at once, we're likely to overload their working memories, causing fatigue, frustration, and forgetfulness. As noted in a previous chapter, neuroscience studies have found that people with post-traumatic stress disorder—including children who have endured psychological trauma—tend to have a smaller hippocampus (Bremner, 2006). As a result, they may struggle to hold information in their working memories. The best way around this limitation—for all students—is pausing frequently during learning to help students mentally cluster information into larger concepts (Bailey & Pransky, 2014).

Our Brains Crave Patterns—for Better or Worse

The good news is that our brains appear to be hardwired to engage in this sort of clustering. Basically, our brains are pattern-making machines. Even children as young as 2 years old look for patterns in their environments. In fact, as Julian Pine, a British professor of early childhood learning, notes, their "clever mistakes"—such as using incorrect words like "go'ed"—are actually quite sensible and reveal that toddlers have observed a pattern, such as adding -ed to regular verbs to make them past tense (2015, p. 22).

The bad news is that our natural aptitude for making patterns can, at times, get us into trouble, especially when we identify nonexistent patterns or jump to mistaken conclusions about what we're observing. Studies have shown, for example, that people often see patterns in what's really just random coincidence. For example, basketball coaches, fans, and players often see a player making several consecutive shots as evidence that player is having a "hot hand" and assume her teammates should all pass the ball to her to let her shoot while her hand remains "hot." An extensive analysis of thousands of sequences of players' shots in basketball games, however, found that there is no such thing as a hot hand: players' shooting streaks never extend beyond what might be expected in tests of randomness—such as the number of times a coin can, by chance, land on the same side (Gilovich, Vallone, & Tversky, 1985).

So, as students begin to make sense of their learning, it's important to be aware that their brains are actively looking to find and make patterns. Some of these patterns will be accurate and helpful; others will not. Hence, it's often at this point in the learning process that students form misconceptions—like assuming phases of the moon are caused by Earth's shadow, acquired traits can be inherited, or blood turns blue in our veins when it loses oxygen.

Because students are so prone to misconceptions, Willingham suggests that teachers "use discovery learning carefully" (2003, p. 80). Yes, learning is often more powerful when students discover it for themselves as opposed to having it "handed to them." Willingham warns, though, that without adequate direction from teachers, "students will remember incorrect 'discoveries' just as well as correct ones" (p. 80). In other words, to ensure students don't form these misconceptions, we need to make student thinking visible and help students make accurate sense of what they're learning.

Our Brains Need Occasional Time-Outs

Here's a third big idea: like MacGyver working against the clock of a ticking time bomb, our working memories tend to time out after 5–10 minutes for preadolescents and 10–20 minutes for adults (Sousa, 2011). Recall that, as cognitive scientist Daniel Kahneman (2011) notes, our brains are lazy and eager to revert back to "low-effort mode." Sure, we can try to fight this tendency, but doing so requires a great deal of effort and willpower—more than most are willing to expend.

This idea suggests it's important to design brief mental breaks into student learning, "chunking" learning into shorter segments, with opportunities for mental processing between each interval. In short, our brains need frequent changes of pace—opportunities to pause and cluster what we've been learning into bigger concepts or categories, to focus momentarily on something else, or to simply change our emotional states. Brain science tells us, in fact, that these breaks for processing need to be fairly frequent—about every 10 minutes or so. This rule seems to be fairly ironclad. If we don't get these breaks, our brains are apt to take them anyway, checking out mentally.

In hindsight, I saw this principle at work while teaching in high school and college classrooms. Of course, I didn't fully recognize what I was seeing before I learned the "chunking" principle. All I knew is I dreaded teaching 90-minute classes; I'd see eyes glaze over and blame myself—or my students—for their lack of engagement. What was really happening, of course, is their overtaxed brains needed a short break to process what they were learning.

Truth be told, I still use this principle at work in my current "classrooms"—providing adult learning in workshops and keynote sessions. I've learned that if I ever violate this "rule"—such as seeing I've got 20 minutes until lunch and deciding to power on through to the break—I *always* regret it. My audience's eyes begin to glaze over, and people start sneaking peeks at their smartphones, looking for a diversion or way to give their brains a break.

We Only Encode What We Think About

Decades ago, Thomas Hyde and James Jenkins conducted a now-classic experiment in which they asked college students to listen to a list of 24 words. Some participants were asked to rate the words as to whether they had pleasant or unpleasant connotations (e.g., *garbage* is unpleasant); others were asked to simply count the number of letters in the word or the instances of the letter *e* in them. Afterward, researchers found that students who thought about the pleasantness or unpleasantness of the words could recall one-third more words than those who focused on letters (Hyde & Jenkins, 1969). In an added twist, the lists also included highly associated words (e.g., *doctor-nurse*) that weren't necessarily listed together. Nonetheless, when recalling words, those who focused on connotations tended to cluster 67.5 percent of the words, whereas students who hadn't focused on meaning only clustered 26.3 percent.

Again, we see that what we think about when we encounter new knowledge has a great deal to do with how information gets stored in our memories. To learn anything, students must concentrate on the meaning—the why, how, and connections—of what they're learning.

Learning by Making Connections

At the heart of sense making—*all* learning, really—is connecting what we're learning with what we already know. As a result, the less prior knowledge we have, they more trouble we have making sense of our learning. Imagine, for example, opening a newspaper and reading this article:

> Cheteshwar Pujara's third century of the series has lifted India to 4-303 at stumps on day one of the fourth Test in Sydney, where Australia failed to strike with the second new ball. Pujara finished 130 not out at stumps on Thursday, when his highest score of a career-best series significantly boosted India's bid for a maiden Test series win in Australia. (Horne, 2019)

If you're a typical American reader, you're bewildered. What are they talking about? It's in English, but why doesn't it make sense? You can probably surmise it's describing some kind of contest . . . the article mentions balls . . . sports, maybe? Why can't we grasp the overall idea and meaning of what we're reading?

It's because we lack prior knowledge. We're unable to relate what we're reading to any sort of mental models already existing in our brains. On the other hand, if you're from India, Australia, England, or any other country where cricket is a popular sport, the article makes perfect sense. If you're from one of these countries, swapping the sample article for one that describes the outcome of an American baseball game might be equally puzzling. (*Sacrifice fly? What the heck is that? Sounds gruesome!*)

Or consider an economics graph (see Figure 5.1). If we lack prior knowledge about economic principles, we may simply see two lines intersecting each other but not understand what it's showing us. However, if someone explains what we're seeing—that the horizontal axis shows quantity (*Oh, right . . . how much stuff is out there*) and the vertical axis shows price (*OK, how much stuff costs*)—and then explains how the descending line on the graph shows prices dropping as supply increases and the ascending line shows prices rising as demand increases, intersecting at equilibrium price, then we can grasp the learning

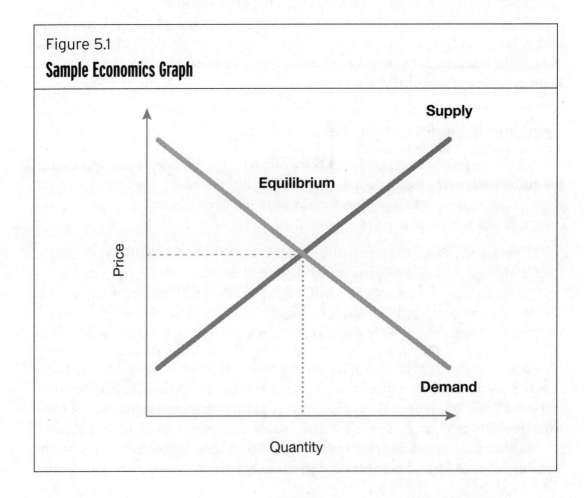

Figure 5.1
Sample Economics Graph

shared with us. Even better, someone might help us relate the abstract graph to everyday experience—for example, bargains at an outlet mall reflecting excess supply of last season's shoes. (*Oh . . . that's why all the neon green sneakers are on sale. Quantity exceeds demand.*)

Switching Up Learning Keeps Our Brains Engaged

As students' brains begin to time out, what often brings them back to learning is an anecdote, a funny video, or time to chat with one another. The breaks are particularly powerful if they help learners adjust the knobs, so to speak, on their emotional states—which, incidentally, is a classic screenwriting technique. The building blocks of movies are short (about 10 minutes long) segments called scenes. According to screenwriting guru Robert McKee (1997), well-written scenes always "turn"—that is, [they switch from one emotional state to its opposite.] Happy turns sad. Safe turns fearful. Bleak turns hopeful. Hate turns to love. For example, a scene might begin with a man walking home from work beneath a blue sky, whistling a tune, and waving happily to neighbors. He pushes open his front door and loses his grip on his briefcase. His home is devoid of furniture and his eyes are drawn to a note on the kitchen counter: "I'm leaving you, John." Wham: the scene has turned, and the film has held our interest—at least for another 10 minutes or so.

These little roller coasters of emotion, as it turns out, reflect brain science. To stay interested in what we're watching, learning, or reading, our brains need new stimuli—often those with a different emotional valence—that allow us to remain connected to what we're learning or to connect to it in a different way. For example, if you've been engaged in a serious conversation in your classroom, you might switch to a more light-hearted personal story.

Or picture this: You're reading a book about the science of learning. You've been at it for several minutes. It's pretty heavy stuff—brain science and all. Your own brain is getting tired, so your mind starts to drift even as your eyes keep moving over the page. You're on autopilot, not really absorbing the book. But then, the author offers an anecdote about screenwriting, relating it to the classroom. It's unexpected, and you've learned something new. Maybe you feel a little differently about "chunking" lessons and providing some variety in them. You're back, ready to read on.

Welcome back. Shall we continue? While we're at it, let's switch gears again to consider what all of this means for your classroom.

Make Sense of Learning: A Classroom Toolkit

These principles of encoding point to a number of tried-and-true strategies we can build into the design of lessons and units to help students cluster and connect learning into meaningful patterns. As with other strategies in other toolkits, it's likely that you already use many of these in your classroom. Yet as with the other phases of learning, seeing how these strategies can support students in processing and making sense of what they're learning will help you use them even more effectively and efficiently in your classroom.

"Chunk" Learning into Segments to Support Processing

As you design learning experiences for students, it's important to provide them with opportunities to pause and process what they're learning. That means making connections, finding similarities and differences, and thinking and talking about their learning with others. A good rule of thumb to follow here is 5 minutes for young learners and up to a maximum of 10 minutes for older learners. If you find yourself talking for more than about 10 minutes, it's probably time to pause and let students process what they're learning. Your students' brains will thank you for it. Of course, this doesn't mean you're taking a pause from learning—far from it. Rather, you're giving students an opportunity to encode what they're learning into memory. As you'll see, you can draw from several research-based strategies to help students engage in productive pauses.

Ask Probing Questions

Teachers spend an estimated 35–50 percent of class asking questions, which adds up to some 300–400 questions per day (Leven & Long, 1981). However, in many classrooms, the bulk of these questions tend to be low-level recall questions. Moreover, instead of facilitating active classroom dialogue, teachers tend to be the ones asking all the questions, and students passively respond to them. Asking the wrong types of questions can turn classrooms into something that resembles a television game show with only a handful of students regurgitating answers to questions no one cares much about while the rest of the class tunes out. The right questions, though, can bring all students into the conversation and make your classroom a vibrant learning environment where students explore ideas, think deeply about learning, and learn to ask their own questions.

Meta-analyses of hundreds of research studies have, in fact, confirmed that when used correctly, questions can be an incredibly powerful teaching technique (Beesley & Apthorp, 2010; Marzano, 1998; Schroeder, Scott, Tolson, Huang, & Lee, 2007; Sencibaugh, 2007), especially when students learn to ask their own questions—that is, drawing on their own curiosity about what they're learning (Rosenshine, Meister, & Chapman, 1996). Recall that during this phase of learning, we want students to think about what they're learning. Good questions help them activate prior learning, see how ideas connect, understand how things work and why, and examine their preconceptions (and misconceptions) about what they're learning (Bransford, Brown, & Cocking, 2000). We can help students develop these deeper insights by asking probing questions, including *why*, *how*, *what if*, and *how do you know* questions (Pomerance et al., 2016).

To do this well, we must preplan our questions—identify beforehand how we'll engage students in thinking about their learning. Figure 5.2 provides several types (based loosely on Bloom's [1956] taxonomy) and stems for questions that help students make sense of their learning.

Figure 5.2
Deeper Questions and Question Stems

Type	Purpose	Question Stems
Comprehension and understanding	Help students connect ideas, including new learning to prior learning.	• How would you describe . . . in your own words? • How is this similar to (or different from) . . . ? • How would you explain why . . . ?
Application and transfer	Encourage students to use their learning in new ways.	• Where else might you apply this . . . ? • What personal connection can you draw to . . . ? • What approach would you use to . . . ?
Analysis and relationships	Encourage students to make inferences and identify relationships.	• How is . . . similar to . . . ? • What is the relationship between . . . ? • How would you categorize . . . ?
Synthesis and creation	Prompt creative perspectives, solutions to problems, or predictions.	• What's a better way to . . . ? • What's a possible solution to . . . ? • What do you think would happen if . . . ?
Evaluation questions	Students make judgments about information or validity of ideas.	• How would you convince someone that . . . ? • Do you think it's a good/bad idea to . . . ? • What would you have done if . . . ?

Try This: No Hands Up

Research has shown that in many classrooms, a few students tend to dominate conversations—following something close to an 80-20 rule, with 20 percent of students responsible for 80 percent of the interactions with teachers.

That means most students are likely doing little to process what they're learning. To engage all students in making sense of their learning, replace undirected questions (posing questions to the whole class and calling only on volunteers with their hands up) with directed questions (calling on individual students to answer questions) (Walsh & Sattes, 2005).

One way to do this is an approached developed by British teacher Pam Fearnley and championed by Dylan Wiliam (McGill, 2011) called *pose, pause, pounce, bounce.* First, you pose a question to all students, then after pausing for three-plus seconds of wait time, "pounce" on one student to answer the question, and "bounce" the question (again using wait time) to another student.

These kinds of deeper questions, however, are often not common in many classrooms. Studies have found, for example, that in most classrooms, roughly 60 percent of questions are low-level, 20 percent are high-level, and 20 percent are procedural (Cotton, 1998). A barrage of such questions rarely engages students in deeper learning. It's far better to ask fewer well-placed, more thoughtful questions that may be more challenging to plan for but ultimately save you time and get better results, since you needn't come up with a lot of them.

Provide Wait Time After Questions

A second idea closely related to deeper questions is simply this: wait a few seconds after asking a question and again after students respond to the question before calling on another student. While listening to hours of recorded student-teacher interactions, Mary Budd Rowe (1986) heard student-teacher dialogue occurring in rapid-fire fashion in most classrooms. Teachers peppered students with questions, and students responded quickly with short, clipped, and typically unsophisticated answers. In a handful of classrooms, though, long pauses followed teachers' questions before students responded. As result, students were more deliberate with their answers, taking time to gather their thoughts. Rowe began using a stopwatch to measure these after-question pauses (what she called "wait time") and found that when they extended for three seconds or more—both after teachers' questions and following students' responses—students' responses were *three to seven times* longer than in classrooms where teachers provided hardly any wait time at all.

Moreover, Rowe found that when teachers avoided cutting off students' responses (waiting a few seconds after each response), they were more likely to support their responses with evidence and logical arguments. Interestingly, in the longer wait-time classrooms, students also began asking their own questions, generating hypotheses and proposing new experiments and interaction with one another in rich dialogue. In addition, Rowe observed that in classrooms with short wait times, most interactions came from only a handful of students, who, like game show contestants, were ready to "buzz in" with answers to teachers' questions. In longer wait-time classrooms, many more students participated. Rowe also observed that wait times helped students feel more engaged and curious about their own learning. She quoted a 5th grader whose teacher used longer wait times as saying, "It's the first time in all my years in school that anybody cared about what I really thought—not just what I'm supposed to say" (1986, p. 44). As Rowe put it, "Under the longer wait time schedule, some previously 'invisible' people become visible" (p. 45).

Use Cooperative Groups to Support Processing

Before diving into cooperative learning as a learning strategy, I must admit, as a teacher, I used to think it was a dumb idea. For starters, as a student, I'd seen so-called cooperative learning turn into one or two kids doing all the work while the others freeloaded (I know, because I was one of the freeloaders). As a teacher, I'd seen group work come off the rails—turning into noisy classrooms where it was unclear if anyone was actually learning.

Therefore, I understand if you have your own misgivings or doubts about group work. You may wonder, like me, if it really works. Yet as Bransford and colleagues (2000) note in their seminal book *How People Learn*, asking whether a strategy like cooperative learning works better than, say, individual learning is really the "wrong" question to ask—akin "to asking which tool is best—a hammer, a screwdriver, a knife, or pliers?" (p. 22). The better question to ask is *when* does a strategy like cooperative learning work best?

As it turns out, one of the best times to employ cooperative learning is right now, during this phase of learning, when students are processing what they're learning—which is to say, what you've likely taught them during the focus on new learning phase of learning. That's because, for starters, human beings are social learners—from our earliest days asking our neighbors how to start a fire to modern times asking friends if the new pizza parlor in town is any good.

Research shows, in fact, that a key benefit of cooperative learning is that it provides students with an opportunity to "talk through" material with their peers and thus learn it in a deeper and richer way than individual reading or listening (Johnson, Maruyama, Johnson, Nelson, & Skon, 1981). Talking through ideas or solutions for problems helps students become more conscious of the strategies they use to get to an answer and better retain new knowledge and skills later. In other words, peer conversations are a great way to help students process or make sense of learning yet an ineffective way to encounter new learning (Stevens, Slavin, & Farnish, 1991).

As my colleagues and I observe classrooms, though, we often see students doing group work that has, at best, only a vaguely defined purpose—for example, sitting in small groups reading a book chapter together. In other words, we see students engaging in cooperative learning during the focus on new learning phase of their learning, when strategies such as direct instruction, modeling, and interleaving worked problems with unsolved problems function better. In other words, teachers may be using the "right" strategy at the wrong time—akin to using pliers to insert a nail into a board.

As a teacher, it's important to regularly ask questions such as "Why am I asking students to work in groups? What do I want them to be thinking and talking about when working in groups? What will they be learning or doing together that they could not do as effectively individually or as a whole class?" Keeping these questions in mind, here are some tried-and-true activities that help students make sense of learning in cooperative groups:

- **Socratic seminar.** After close reading of a text, ask students to sit in a circle. Provide thoughtful, open-ended questions to help them think about their learning (e.g., "What is the author's perspective? Do you have a different perspective?"). Using the pose, pause, pounce, bounce approach, you can engage every student in rich dialogue to identify key ideas, analyze arguments, and discuss students' feelings about the text.
- **Final-word protocol.** This small-group discussion strategy works best with texts or learning that invites multiple viewpoints. In groups of four, each student spends one minute answering a high-order question that you provide, while other students listen and take notes. After a minute,

another student shares his or her thoughts while the others take notes. The last student to speak in each round gets the "final word." The order is switched in subsequent rounds so every student can speak last. After four rounds, the groups identify three key issues to share with the whole class.

- **Legalized note passing.** In this simple strategy, students write short responses to thought-provoking questions and pass their responses back and forth to one another.
- **Think-pair-share.** Pose a high-order question to students. Then ask them to reflect on it (and perhaps offer a written response) and share their thoughts with their neighbors.
- **Reciprocal teaching.** After students independently read a text, create groups of four students who each have one role: summarizer, questioner, clarifier, and predictor. Students take turns guiding the discussion according to their designated role as groups help one another make sense of the text.

Help Students Identify Similarities and Differences

Comparing and contrasting is a vitally important thinking skill that helps students make sense of what they're learning by clustering and categorizing concepts. For example, students might categorize main characters from novels they've read based on personalities, motivations, strengths, and weaknesses or identifying common political, cultural, and economic conditions that lead to revolutions. Research shows that the mental process of identifying similarities and differences helps learners gain new insights, draw inferences, extract generalizations, and refine mental models (Holyoak, 2005). Showing students how concepts contrast with one another also helps them notice new features and identify which features are most relevant to a concept (Bransford et al., 2000). For example, they might see that an oligarchy shares many of the same features of a dictatorship (i.e., concentrating power) with an important difference—concentrating power in the hands of a few people versus just one.

In *Classroom Instruction That Works* (Dean et al., 2012), we described similarities and differences as a broad category of instructional strategies composed of the following teaching (and thinking) strategies:

- **Comparing** identifies similarities between or among things or ideas (e.g., ducks and penguins are both aquatic birds).
- **Contrasting** identifies differences between or among things or ideas (e.g., ducks can fly; penguins cannot).

- **Classifying** groups things into categories based on shared characteristics (e.g., ducks and penguins both belong to the bird family).
- **Creating metaphors** identifies a general or basic pattern in a concept, then finds the same general pattern in another topic that initially seems different (e.g., ducks are like seaplanes since they can both fly and land on water).
- **Creating analogies** identifies relationships between pairs of concepts, showing *A* is to *B* as *C* is to *D* (e.g., ducks are to penguins as seaplanes are to amphibious vehicles).

By helping students connect prior knowledge to new knowledge, parse differences among similar ideas, and move from concrete examples to abstract ideas (and vice versa), these strategies help students make sense of learning, using what they already know as a springboard to more deeply process new learning.

Researchers note, in fact, that these mental processes are in many ways the core of all learning (Bransford et al., 2000; Chen, 1999; Fuchs et al., 2006; Gentner, Loewenstein, & Thompson, 2003; Holyoak, 2005). Basically, when we learn anything new, our brains must ask, "How is this like what I already know?" In so doing, we create a mental model for what we've learned (e.g., all birds have wings) or add new learning to an existing mental model (e.g., all birds have wings, but not all birds fly).

Two McREL meta-analyses have identified—and confirmed—this strategy as one of the most powerful tools you can use in your classroom (Beesley & Apthorp, 2010; Marzano, 1998), with an effect size that equates to scoring 25 percentile points higher on a standardized test. However, it's important that teachers guide these processes. To wit: activating students' prior knowledge *without* helping them make connections between new and prior learning has only middling effects on their learning (Ling, Chik, & Pang, 2006; Schwartz et al., 2006).

Similarly, simply asking students to create analogies without guidance or teacher-provided examples has little or no effect on learning (BouJaoude & Tamin, 1998). On the other hand, providing students with opportunities for teacher-guided reflection and discussion with peers of analogies has been found to have significant effects on learning (Baser & Geban, 2007; Chen, 1999; Mbajiorgu et al., 2006; Rule & Furletti, 2004). All these findings suggest you have an important role to play as a teacher in helping students make connections between prior learning and new learning as well as in guiding them and engaging them in discussions that help them make sense of learning.

Invite Students to Summarize Their Learning

Another mental process that appears to be essential to make sense of learning is summarizing what we've learned. Studies show that when students summarize new learning—that is, when they sort, select, combine, and rephrase information—they significantly improve their comprehension (Boch & Piolat, 2005). In fact, summarizing is likely what makes note taking such a powerful strategy. While taking notes, students must sift through what they're hearing and observing to identify a few key ideas, arrange them in a sensible manner, and encode them by writing them down. So it's perhaps not surprising that McREL's meta-analysis of research on instruction (Beesley & Apthorp, 2010) found that summarizing is particularly effective when combined with note taking, which had a greater effect on learning (0.90) than summarizing alone (0.32).

It's worth noting, however, that summarizing has a greater effect on learning when teachers provide students with direct guidance for summarizing—showing, for example, how to identify key ideas from a lecture or reading, group them, and distill them into main points (Kobayashi, 2006). Like many other strategies, summarizing is often most effective when combined with other strategies. Like protein powder added to a smoothie, summarizing appears to be a key ingredient within note taking, reciprocal teaching, and elaborative rehearsal (which we'll discuss in the next chapter). Here are some ways to help students engage in summarizing to make sense of their learning:

- **Teach students how to summarize.** Giving students rules or steps to follow when summarizing helps demystify the process. Specifically, show students how to (1) remove material that doesn't support understanding, (2) ignore redundant information, (3) replace lists with categorical descriptors (e.g., replace *ducks*, *penguins*, and *eagles* with *birds*), and (4) locate or draft a topic sentence or thesis statement.
- **Provide students with summary frames.** Studies show helping students see how information is structured helps them better summarize and remember new material (Broer, Aarnoutse, Kieviet, & van Leeuwe, 2002; Meyer et al., 2002; Meyer & Poon, 2001). One way to do this is to give students "summary frames" or questions that highlight key elements for specific types of text, as shown in Figure 5.3.
- **Engage students in writing tasks that synthesize learning.** In keeping with the adage that "I don't know what I think until I know what I write," studies have found that writing supports deeper thinking about

Figure 5.3
Summary Frames and Questions

Type	Questions	Examples
Narrative	• Who are the main characters? • When/where does the story take place? • What conflict prompts the action in the story? • How do the main characters respond to the conflict? • What are the results or consequences?	• Montresor and Fortunato • In Montresor's catacombs • Montresor wants revenge for something Fortunato said/did (we don't know what). • Fortunato doesn't realize he's in danger until it's too late. • Montresor buries Fortunato alive.
Topic-Restriction-Illustration	• T: What is the general statement/topic? • R: What information restricts or narrows general statement or topic? • I: What examples illustrate restriction?	• Fish • Fish have backbones and are cold-blooded; most have gills, scales, and fins. • Dolphins are warm-blooded—thus, not fish.
Definition	• What is being defined? • To which category does it belong? • What characteristics separate it from other things in the general category? • What are some different types or classes of the item being defined?	• Oligarchy • . . . is a type of government • . . . that represents rule of few versus rule of many or just one • Kleptocracies are often oligarchies; those in power are corrupt or criminal.
Argumentation	• Claim: What basic statement or claim is being made? • Evidence: What examples or explanations support the claim? • Qualifier: What restricts the claim, or what evidence counters the claim?	• Casinos create an unfair, regressive tax on poor people. • Most patrons have low incomes and have gambling problems. • Casinos provide jobs and income for many, including disadvantaged populations.
Problem solving	• What is the problem? • What is a possible solution? • What is another possible solution? • Which solution has the best chance of succeeding and why?	• Plastic straws harm aquatic life. • We could ban straws. • We could switch to biodegradable straws. • Using biodegradable straws because it's easier to alter than eliminate a habit.
Conversation	• What questions were asked? • Were facts were stated and/or disputed? • Were requests/demands were made? • Were praise/compliments were offered? • How did the conversation conclude?	• Interviewer asked about kids using product. • CEO said company doesn't market to them. • Interviewer noted product has flavors that appeal to kids and asked for apology. • CEO said he's sorry for kids but hasn't done anything wrong.

Source: From *Classroom Instruction That Works: Research-Based Strategies for Increasing Student Achievement* (2nd ed) by C. B. Dean, E. R. Hubbell, H. Pitler, & B. Stone, 2012, Alexandria, VA: ASCD. Copyright 2012 by McREL. Adapted with permission.

new learning. For example, Langer and Applebee (1987) provided early evidence in a small but in-depth study to suggest well-designed writing assignments support deeper processing of new learning. They monitored six students using think-alouds to hear what students thought about while reading and reviewing a social studies text using note taking, study questions, and an analytical essay. When answering study questions, students engaged in fragmented, low-level recognition and recall. When taking notes, they focused on more content yet failed to integrate it into bigger ideas. Only when writing an essay did they engage in critical thinking—synthesizing, hypothesizing, and evaluating ideas.

The Big Idea: Taking the Time to Make Sense of Learning

It's worth noting that the best way to help students make sense of their learning isn't to show them how new ideas or skills are categorized, juxtaposed, or linked to their prior learning but, rather, to engage them in asking their own processing questions about what they're learning—for example, "How do these ideas connect? How are they different? How is this new skill like (or unlike) something I can already do?" Here again, you're tapping into their own natural curiosity to help them make these connections.

Of course, for some teachers, taking the time to chunk learning into segments and pausing to let students make sense of their learning may seem like a luxury you can ill afford—especially if you feel like you already have too much to cover or an administrator waving a pacing guide at you. If you feel this way, pause a moment to make sense yourself of what might be happening.

For starters, you might look again at everything you're trying to shoehorn into a lesson—is it all necessary? Or can you prune some of the breadth in favor of depth? Similarly, you might look at your pacing. Are you allocating (or inadvertently spending) too much time on topics or skills you could introduce or model more efficiently? We often have favorite ideas, anecdotes, and activities we love to use, but sometimes, on further reflection, we see they may not be the most effective or efficient way to help students learn. So we may be able to pick up the pace in earlier phases of learning—for example, being a little less clever or time intensive in how we help students become interested in learning and/or spending less time engaged in direct teaching during the focus on new learning phase to carve out more time for students to make sense of learning.

If you've done that and still feel like you have no time to let students pause and process, we encourage you to share this book and its research with your colleagues or administrators, engaging them in a conversation about the importance of giving students time to make sense of their learning—especially in light of the fact that students tend to forget 90 percent of what they learn in school within 30 days of learning it (Medina, 2008). So it might be worth asking, "If we taught less (but at more depth), might students actually learn more?" Together with your colleagues, you'll hopefully be able to identify some topics or areas to trim from the curriculum so you can engage your students in deeper learning that sticks.

After all, giving students ample time to make sense of learning is critical to their comprehension, recall, and ability to engage in deep learning and help them take more after MacGyver than MacGruber, piecing together what they are learning before time runs out.

6

Practice and Reflect

You've probably all had the experience of returning to a familiar place after a long absence, such as an old neighborhood or home. Within moments of turning on to our old street or stepping into the house, you likely experienced many long-forgotten memories pop back into your consciousness. The names of neighbors and old friends. Lovers' initials carved into tree trunks. The smell of your grandmother's cookies. Sometimes, the whole experience and onslaught of memories—joyful, sad, wistful—can be overpowering.

A few years ago, I had such an experience when I returned, after a 25-year hiatus, to the campus of my alma mater. After college, my life's journey carried me away from the town, state, and region where I'd gone to school, never to return until my eldest daughter expressed a desire to visit on a college tour. Eagerly, I agreed to join her. Within minutes of returning to campus, a flood of memories— names of classmates, professors, fraternity brothers, and other friends whom I hadn't thought about for years—came rushing back to me. Some memories were funny—my pals earnestly attempting to communicate with the on-campus mascot (a live bear) with Chewbacca noises—and some were sad, such as lamenting unrequited love beneath a sprawling magnolia tree in the moonlight.

I realized a funny thing, though, when I texted some of my college buddies to reminisce (and LOL!) about some of our sophomoric hijinks. Surprisingly, although some memories were now in high-def resolution in my memory, my college friends didn't remember many of them. When they texted back their own memories, they'd sometimes jar loose a long-forgotten memory in me, but just as often, I had no recollection of their memories. And no, adult beverages had (mostly) nothing to do with our hazy recollections. We had simply retained different memories.

As we'll see in the next two chapters, how our brains store and later retrieve long-term memories can be a frustratingly inconsistent and inscrutable process.

With limited effort, some memories get indelibly etched into our minds, including some we'd sooner forget (an annoying song, an unkindness that still stings, a regrettable remark of our own). Meanwhile, other memories, including those we yearn to retain, wilt like blossoms on a magnolia (the sound of our grandpa's laugh, where we left our house keys, or what Shakespeare play includes the quote about "a green-ey'd monster").

Some memories remain buried in the recesses of our mind until jogged loose by an associated memory (like crossing a sidewalk and suddenly recalling a bizarre incident of a squirrel running into my bike as I pedaled across campus years before). Other memories, despite our best efforts, simply won't appear ("Sorry, guys, I don't remember the kid with socks and sandals in the back row of our Philosophy 101 class"), making us wonder how they faded—or if we simply failed to record them in the first place.

So why does any of this matter to us educators? Well, because we are in the business of helping students turn information into memories, and we hope what we teach students in our classrooms today sticks with them tomorrow and far into the future. As noted earlier, studies have found that students tend to forget as much as 90 percent of what they learn in school *within a month* (Medina, 2008). You likely experienced this phenomenon yourself as a student when you had to restudy something for a final exam you had learned a month or two earlier. And you've likely experienced the frustration of trying to burn something into memory that won't stick (the precedent established by *Plessy v. Ferguson* or the lines that precede "Told by an idiot, full of sound and fury").

Why should this happen? Why should some memories stick and others fade? How is it we can store some memories but not *retrieve* them, or recall them only after it's too late, like just after that final exam?

As we'll see, much of what we think we know about how to embed new learning into our brains for later retrieval is often wrong. Sometimes, the process can be simpler than we imagine, and other times, it's far more complex. As we'll explore, a key principle at work here is that *storing* and *retrieving* memories are actually two different processes that require different procedures and conditions to make them happen. We'll unpack how to help our students store information in their brains as well as retrieve it for later use. More specifically, we'll identify some tried-and-true ways to protect new memories from something akin to an overzealous night janitor that makes its way through our brains (often as we sleep), sweeping out what it deems to be useless information.

The Science of Embedding Memories

At this point in the learning process, you've helped your students become interested and committed to learning. They've also absorbed new information by focusing on new learning and have begun to cluster and consolidate that information into coherent patterns to make sense of learning. The journey, however, is not done. Now we must help students embed learning into their memories so they can recall it later. Let's start by taking a close look at what it takes to deposit new learning in our memory banks, ensuring it stays in the vault so we can withdraw it later.

Repeat, Repeat, Repeat

Basically, whether new learning finds a permanent home in our long-term memory depends on whether our brains go on more than one date, so to speak, with the new learning. As described in the last chapter, we don't store memories neatly in a single neuron or in a tidy corner of our brains; rather, they're splattered across our brains in a messy network of neurons connected by neural pathways. When we *return* to that memory, we reactivate all the pathways that connect those neurons together. As we reactivate them, our brains begin to wrap a sheath of insulation (called myelin) around those neural pathways. Just like insulation around an electrical wire that helps electrical charges move more quickly, that myelin coating makes it easier for us to fire up those neurons again.

All this leads us to our first key principle of memory storage: repeat, repeat, repeat.

Basically, there's no getting around this rule. If you want to remember something, you must repeat the memory in your mind—multiple times. Studies suggest, for example, that students need to rehearse a new skill at least 24 times before they reach 80 percent competency (Anderson, 1995).

Yet as we'll see, just like any process, the *quality* of those repetitions is as important (if not more important) than the quantity. Yes, you need to go on more than one date with your new bit of learning, but like any successful courtship, they should be *good* dates of increasing complexity (moving from superficial to deeper connections) and not simply a repeat of previous experiences. (*Dinner and a movie . . . again?*)

As it turns out, simply repeating new knowledge or a skill right after learning it is necessary, but not sufficient, for long-term recall. For example, if you want to say "good morning" in a foreign language, it's often helpful to repeat it many times until you feel comfortable saying it to a stranger—which, incidentally, is something I do when I travel abroad for work. I cram a handful of go-to words and phrases from the local language into my vocabulary like *hello, good-bye,* and *thank you.* All too often, though, my expanded vocabulary evaporates as soon as I return home.

My poor retention of these phrases reflects an important maxim of practice: although cramming leads to better short-term retention of new learning, it's an ephemeral sort of learning. As two cognitive scientists who studied the results of cramming put it, "Procedures that produce fast learning can produce fast forgetting" (Roediger & Pyc, 2012, p. 244), which leads us to our next principle for storing new learning in long-term memory.

"Re-Wetting" the Concrete with Spaced Practice

Studies dating back to Hermann Ebbinghaus (1885), whom you met in Chapter 1, have shown that the best way to encode learning into long-term memory is to space practice sessions over a period of days or even weeks. Cramming, it turns out, may be the best way to learn something in the short term, yet it's the *worst* way to retain it in the long term. For example, when researchers asked two groups of high school students to study 20 French-English vocabulary pairs (e.g., *l'avocat-lawyer*)—the first in a single, intense 30-minute bout of study, and the second in three 10-minute sessions spread over three consecutive days—the two groups performed comparably on a quiz given at the end of the week (Bloom & Shuell, 1981). Yet when retested (with no further practice) just four days later, the spaced practice group performed significantly better, having retained most of the new vocabulary, whereas the massed practice group forgot roughly one-third of the vocabulary they had "known" just days before.

Repeated practice sessions over a period of several days help students more deeply encode new learning into their brains. Cognitive scientists believe that's because massed practice may facilitate *retrieval* but not *storage* of new learning (Bjork & Bjork, 2011). Basically, repeating in a single session forges a path in our minds that only creates an "illusion of knowing" (Brown et al., 2014). We *think* we have new knowledge etched into our memories, but it's a little like knowing only one route to an unfamiliar place—if we get turned around or find ourselves a block off the beaten path, we get lost.

However, if we rehash fresh memories in repeated sessions spaced out over time, our brains reactivate the original neural network used to encode them, thereby returning the memory to its original impressionable state, which allows our brains to connect additional ideas, emotions, and memories to it. This creates an even more complex web, which makes the new learning more deeply embedded and *stored* in our memories (Medina, 2008).

For example, when we first encounter the word pair *l'avocat-lawyer*, we might focus on seeing and saying the foreign word simultaneously, thereby creating a visual memory of the word. On day two, as we picture the word and recall its pronunciation in our minds, we reinforce both connections; at the same time, we might recall that our Aunt Anna is a lawyer and connect her face and name with the word: *Anna l'avocat*. On day three, as we return to the word, seeing and hearing it in our minds along with an image of Anna (further reinforcing all the neural connections), we might also remember that she has a cat and create a memory device (called a mnemonic) to remember the word: *Anna l'avocat loves a cat*. A few days later, when we're presented with a pop quiz asking us for the French word for *lawyer*, *l'avocat* is likely to spring easily to mind.

All this is important because cognitive scientists have found that the more associations we make with a new memory, the more likely we will be able to store and retrieve it for later use (Medina, 2008). By "re-wetting" the concrete, so to speak, of the learning we may have initially cemented in our minds in a simple and superficial way, we're better able to retain and retrieve it later. Sure, we might have made all these associations with *l'avocat* on our first day of study, but then all our associations with the word would have been fragile and likely to fade. It's therefore better to layer those associations.

Mixing Up Practice Makes It Tougher (and Better)

As a teenager, I spent countless hours shooting baskets at a rusting hoop above our garage from a line I'd chalked across the driveway to be the same distance as a regulation free throw line. Over and over, I'd shoot the same shot, hoping to improve my free throw percentage (and chances of making the basketball team). If my shot fell short, I'd put a little more oomph on the next one. If that shot slammed against the backboard or drifted left, I'd adjust the following shot accordingly, all while standing in the same spot in the driveway—sometimes for as many as 100 shots (making it easy to tabulate my percentage).

Despite my diligence, I didn't make the basketball team. I'm sure being a 90-pound weakling had something to do with it, but now, in hindsight, so did my approach to practice, which research shows was, in many ways, exactly the *wrong* approach. Despite being spaced over the year, my muscle memory would've improved a whole lot faster not by taking the same shot but, rather, by moving around my driveway and shooting from different locations, engaging in something researchers call *interleaving practice*.

Kerr and Booth (1978) observed 64 8- and 12-year-olds in a study that asked one group to practice throwing beanbags into a bucket three feet away and another group to practice from alternating distances two and four feet away. After 12 weeks, the group practicing from alternating distances outperformed the other group on a final test that asked them throw the beanbags into a bucket from three feet away—a distance they had never practiced, whereas the other group had practiced from that distance exclusively.

Why is that? Researchers believed that by mixing up their practice, the second group developed a better, more robust understanding or feel for the activity—figuring out the best arc, velocity, and hand movement for tossing the beanbag at both distances, which made them more competent at tossing it from any distance.

Subsequent studies have found that this general principle also applies to academic learning. Initial learning is sometimes slower with interleaving practice, yet it nonetheless significantly improves performance over simply practicing the same knowledge or skill in repeat sessions (Rohrer & Pashler, 2010). For example, in one study (Taylor & Rohrer, 2010), 4th graders learned how to calculate the number of faces, edges, corners, and angles on prisms based on the number of base sides they had. Afterward, half the students engaged in a traditional block practice session—working the same type of problem before moving on to the next—while the other half engaged in interleaved practice: working different types of problems in mixed fashion.

The next day, when both groups were tested, the block practice group performed better, recalling nearly 100 percent of the learning versus just 70 percent for the interleaved practice group. When tested again a day later, the interleaved practice group outperformed the block practice group and retained even more learning than they had the day before, recalling close to 80 percent of their learning versus less than 40 percent for the blocked practice group. Perhaps most important, when examining student error patterns, researchers noticed that students in the interleaved practice group committed fewer "discrimination errors" in which they mistook one type of problem for another.

In short, it appears that mixing up the skills we're practicing during a single session forces our brains to work harder, make microadjustments, and reflect on what we're doing. For example, we must recalibrate the strength and arc of the basketball shot depending on whether we're shooting from the middle of the driveway, behind a trash can, or near the neighbor's flowerbed. Likewise, when working different types of math problems, we must pause to consider what computational strategy we should use to divide fractions, multiply decimals, or add fractions (or calculate prism angles, edges, and faces). By engaging in what researchers call "desirable difficulties" (Bjork & Bjork, 1992), we develop richer neural pathways to the learning, which improves our performance in real life where we seldom encounter the same type of problem all day long or an opposing team that graciously allows us to always shoot from the same spot on the court.

Generally speaking, interleaved practice appears to be far from the norm in most classrooms (or textbooks, for that matter). Students and their teachers may perceive such practice as being effective, especially as massed practice can create the illusion of having mastered something we haven't. In reality, though, students benefit more from practice that puts their brains to work by forcing them to solve a mixed batch of problems or challenges in a single practice session.

Location, Location, Location

As I revisited my alma mater, I began recalling my favorite study spots on campus—the swing beneath a live oak tree, the library table bathed in the glow of a stained glass window, the desk in a balcony overlooking an atrium in the student union. In an effort to reduce the tedium of studying, I had eschewed the usual advice to find a single, quiet place to study and had instead opted to lug my books around to a slew of secret study spots all over campus. In so doing, I had (inadvertently) employed what cognitive scientists have shown to be one of the more effective ways to deeply encode memories—namely, to learn (and relearn) information in different locations.

As it turns out, *where* we learn something becomes yet another association with the new memory and thus another hook for retrieving it later. For example, when trying to recall the details of Immanuel Kant's "categorical imperative," a memory of reading about Kant in the mottled shade beneath an oak tree may spring to mind, providing us with a helpful hook for retrieving those details from the depths of our minds.

Cognitive scientists discovered this connection between location and memory years ago through some unusual experiments, including one that asked subjects to memorize and later recall a list of 38 unrelated words while scuba diving under 20 feet of water and, alternately, on dry land (Godden & Baddeley, 1975). Researchers found study participants were more likely to recall the words when quizzed on them in the same location where they had learned them and less likely to recall the words when quizzed on them in a different location from where they'd learned them (e.g., learning them underwater and being quizzed on land).

Although such experimental conditions may not have much real-life application, they suggest location cues are important for recalling what we've learned and that the best place to study for an exam may well be the same room in which we plan to take it. One study, for example, found college students were more apt to recall a list of words when they studied them in the same room in which they were tested (Smith, 1982). Yet it also found something else that may be of more use to students—especially those who are unwilling or unable to catburglar their way into an exam room for after-hours study sessions. Students who engaged in study sessions in four different settings demonstrated greater recall of the words than students who engaged in repeated sessions in just one or two rooms—and just as much recall as students who studied in the same room where the test was given—presumably because once students infuse learning with multiple environmental cues, they can recall the words regardless of the setting in which they were examined.

Racking Our Brains to Remember

Another key principle of practice emerged, quite by accident, a century ago as researchers sought to determine exactly how quickly new academic learning faded from people's memories by quizzing people to see how much they could recall of a previously learned body of knowledge (Gates, 1917). The findings were striking in more ways than one. For starters, students often forgot much of what they learned—even just a few weeks after learning it.

Yet these researchers made another, and more important, discovery: They were "contaminating" their own studies with their incessant quizzes. That is, the more frequently they asked study participants to recall a particular topic, the better participants remembered it. Thus, the researchers stumbled onto a powerful idea that, strangely, has been slow to find its way into classrooms: if you want to remember something, force yourself to try and remember it.

As it turns out, the very act of racking our brains for information helps us recall it better later. Cognitive scientists believe that every attempt to retrieve a memory reactivates the neural networks used to store the memory. When we fire those networks again, we further wrap the neurons that connect memories with more myelin, making it easier to retrieve a memory later. Perhaps most important, searching our memories appears to reactivate our neural networks in more powerful ways than simply rehashing, rereading, or reviewing what we've learned. Like massed practice, rereading our notes or hearing a teacher remind us of what we've learned before can create an "illusion of knowing" something that we haven't actually committed to memory (Brown et al., 2014).

Unless we're rereading something after a lengthy lapse in time, simply reading something again for a second or third time in close succession only serves to reactivate the same neural networks but does little to more deeply embed what we're learning. When we reread something already familiar to us, we may even find ourselves parroting back phrases and sentences that make us think we've mastered what we're reading. However, if we were to close the book and ask ourselves something like, "Can I explain to someone else how a covalent bond works?" we may realize we have yet to fully grasp what we've been reading.

Cognitive scientists have a name for this strategy of quizzing ourselves on new learning: retrieval practice. Studies have shown, in fact, that retrieval practice is one of the most effective ways to commit new learning to memory—for students at all grade levels, including preschool (Fritz, Morris, Nolan, & Singleton, 2007), elementary (Karpicke, Blunt, & Smith, 2016), middle school (McDaniel, Agarwal, Huelser, McDermott, & Roediger, 2011), and high school (McDermott, Agarwal, D'Antonio, Roediger, & McDaniel, 2014). In one such study, researchers divided students into three groups. The first read the same text four times in separate sessions, a second group read the text three times and spent one practice session recalling the text (via writing), and a third group read the text once and spent three practice periods recalling it. The results? Students who read the text just once but spent more time on retrieval practice performed *four times better* than the group that read the material four times with no retrieval practice (Karpicke, 2012).

A study of middle school science students further illustrates the power of retrieval practice. For this study, researchers split students into two groups: one that engaged in three review sessions over the course of a semester and another that never reviewed the material but was quizzed on it (with feedback). When both groups of students were tested at the end of the semester, the second group performed significantly better, averaging an *A–* versus a *C+* for students who only reviewed the material (McDaniel et al., 2011).

Granted, with many students already being tested seemingly ad nauseum, you may be reluctant to add yet another test to your classrooms or students' slate of anxieties. The point here, though, is that searching our brains for recently stored information is a powerful learning strategy—not simply a measure of learning. So what we're really talking about here is reframing quizzes as retrieval practice. They need not be formal or even graded (in fact, it's best if they aren't graded at all). Nonetheless, if students come to anticipate regular quizzes of what they're learning when they return to class, studies have shown they will be more apt to focus (and quiz themselves) on what they're learning while learning it (Weinstein, Gilmore, Szpunar, & McDermott, 2014).

Finding and Fixing the Bugs

A final key principle for storing and retrieving new learning—especially skills-based learning—emerges from studies by K. Anders Ericsson, who spent his entire career studying elite performers in a variety of fields, from figure skaters to surgeons to computer programmers. From these studies, Ericsson calculated that these experts all engaged in 10,000 hours of deliberate practice. As Ericsson observed, "Not all practice makes perfect. You need a particular kind of practice—*deliberate* practice—[which] entails considerable, specific, and sustained efforts to do something you can't do well—or even at all" (Ericsson, Prietula, & Cokely, 2007, p. 3).

For example, when researchers compared the practice habits of 24 figure skaters in Canada, including elite skaters (i.e., those on national teams), competitive skaters (i.e., those who planned to compete at the provincial level), and a test group of skaters who had no intention of competing, they found a remarkable difference—not in how much they practiced but in how well they practiced (Deakin & Cobley, 2003).

For the study, they asked all the skaters a variety of questions about how much they enjoyed certain practice activities, the level of effort and concentration each kind of activity required, and which activities they felt were most important to their success. They also asked the skaters to complete seven-day diaries to track how many hours they practiced. These diaries showed that in general, all groups of skaters devoted the same hours per week to practice, so that point did not appear to be the differentiator. The researchers, however, also asked two ice skating professionals to observe three 45- to 60-minute videos of all 24 skaters practicing.

This is where things got interesting.

Observers noticed that the elite skaters were far more efficient with their practice time; they spent only 14 percent of practice time "resting" (which could include talking to friends, standing at the side of the rink, or leaving the ice altogether) versus 31 percent for competitive skaters and 46 percent for noncompetitive skaters. Moreover, how the elite skaters spent their time on the ice was also telling. They spent 68 percent of their practice sessions on challenging jumps and spins. By contrast, competitive skaters devoted 59 percent of practice time to these difficult activities, and noncompetitive skaters were at only 48 percent.

Consider that for a moment. Jumps and spins rank among the most challenging practice activities, according to all the skaters. Learning them can be embarrassing, not to mention painful. You fall a lot. You have to pick yourself up off the ice and start over, doing the moves again and again until you commit them to muscle memory, learning to perform them without even thinking about them. Ericsson concluded from this and other studies that the "single most important difference between . . . amateurs and . . . elite performers is that the future elite performers" devote more of their practice time to those "aspects of their performance that have the most room for improvement" (Ericsson, Roring, & Nandagopal, 2007, pp. 34, 25).

In short, elite performers don't start out perfect; rather, they understand what aspects of their knowledge, abilities, or performance are most lacking and then engage in deliberate practice to close the gap between where they are and where they want to be. That progression requires continuously reflecting on their own knowledge or skills and asking what they need to do to improve. Researchers call this a discrepancy reduction strategy. We might think of it as akin to software programmers deliberately searching for and fixing "bugs"— small glitches in code that, left unchecked, can crash an entire program.

Bringing It All Together

In many ways, what expert figure skaters do during their deliberate practice sessions reflects much of what we've learned so far about effective practice and reflection. For starters, they understand the importance of repetition (they're on the ice several days a week) and spaced practice (they rehearse the same jumps, spins, and connecting steps in multiple sessions spread over several days, weeks, and months). Moreover, during their practice sessions, they rehearse a variety of moves, interleaving their practice and engaging in constant retrieval practice (working to commit their routines for short and long programs to memory). Perhaps most important, they engage in ongoing reflection about their learning, focusing on what they have yet to master. When they fall, they don't simply pick themselves up and mindlessly repeat the failed jump or spin. Rather, they pause to reflect on what exactly went wrong and what they need to do differently next time—asking themselves, for example, *why* they didn't complete a full rotation or *why* they landed with their weight imbalanced. Then they visualize *how* to do the jump differently on the next attempt.

It's important to teach all these techniques to students—repetition, interleaving, retrieval practice, and elaboration—so they can engage in deliberate practice and size up where they are and what they need to do to shore up their mastery of new learning. In the next section, we'll provide you with tools you can use to help students engage in effective deliberate practice and reflection to solidify their learning.

Practice and Reflect: A Classroom Toolkit

At this point in the learning process, your students are interested in what they've learned, committed to learning it, focused on learning, and have spent some time making sense of it. Nevertheless, whether the journey continues— that is, whether the new learning moves from short- to long-term memory— basically comes down to the simple process of repeating, replaying, rehearsing and reflecting on what they've learned. Students must engage in multiple episodes of returning to the new knowledge and practicing new skills to reinforce the neural pathways that have begun to form in their brains.

Often, we think about students doing this during homework assignments. It's worth noting, though, that piling on heaps of homework for homework's sake does little to benefit students. However, *well-designed practice opportunities are invaluable*. A McREL meta-analysis of research found only a small effect size for homework (.13) but a much larger effect for providing practice (.42) (Beesley & Apthorp, 2010). In other words, students doing more homework is, at best, weakly linked to their success in learning, but students engaging in more practice has been shown to have a strong positive link to their success.

Of course, not all practice is created equal. That's why it's important to be clear about the purpose of practice before assigning it to students. Do you want them to develop automaticity with a new skill? Interleave the practice of various skills to help them build new knowledge or skills more slowly yet more deeply? Refresh prior learning before it fades? Refine new knowledge and skills with deliberate, reflective practice?

As with the other strategies described in this book, rest assured that you needn't use every tool in this toolkit with every learning opportunity you provide students. Rather, you should bring your own professional wisdom and experience to bear to find the right tool for the job at hand.

Observe and Guide Initial Practice

Often, as a first step after students focus on and make sense of new learning, they must solidify the new learning in their minds with an initial round of practice—be it applying a skill (e.g., multicolumn addition) or repeating new learning to commit it to memory (e.g., conjugations for the Spanish verb *venir*). In most cases, during these initial efforts to practice or rehearse new learning, students benefit from some direct guidance.

For starters, studies have found that for many students, engaging in a new procedure for the first time can create excessive "cognitive load" as they must simultaneously juggle recalling the steps for the procedure while at the same following the procedure (van Merrienboer & Sweller, 2005). Because our working memories can only hold a limited number of unrelated bits of information at a time, if we make students juggle too many at once, they are apt to become confused, get frustrated, or skip crucial parts of the process. Yes, *some* difficulty is desirable, but too much difficulty, especially when students are still in the early stages of developing a new skill or if the learning has multiple elements, will likely stress students' working memories past the breaking point and hinder their learning (Chen, Castro-Alonso, Paas, & Sweller, 2018).

For example, when students are learning to solve for x in an algebraic equation (e.g., $2x + 5 = 13$), they must hold up to a dozen bits of information in their head at once—each numeral in the equation, the functions, and how they relate to one another. So, when learning a complex new process like this one, students benefit from worked examples as well as from written guidance or reminders about the steps to follow to carry out a process (Frerejean, Brand-Gruwel, & Kirschner, 2013). You might show them, for example, how to cross multiply, how to write a paragraph with a topic sentence and supporting details, or how to balance a chemical equation.

In summary, when teaching students a new process, it's best to demonstrate it with worked examples, walking them through the process a few times and, ideally, giving them some form of written or video guidance they can refer back to during their first few rounds of practice. At the same time, it's important to observe them as they engage in their initial round of practice. Studies show, in fact, that when students are left too much to their own devices during initial practice, they often learn skills incorrectly or develop misconceptions (Kirschner, Sweller, & Clark, 2006).

It's hard to imagine, for example, a tennis coach giving a student a basket of balls and saying, "OK, serve all of these while I go to the pro shack; I'll come back later to see how many made it over the net." Nevertheless, this is often what happens in schools. Students labor in private agony with their homework assignments, unable to ask for guidance from teachers, who in turn don't see what students are struggling to comprehend or what mistakes they are making as they practice. It's important to observe students during their initial attempts to acquire a new skill or commit new learning to memory.

Check for Understanding

Observing students during their initial practice attempts also helps us check their understanding. Do they know how to carry or replace digits when performing multicolumn addition or subtraction problems? Do they really know what *bourgeoisie* means when reading about the French Revolution?

Try This: Ask Revealing Questions

Here are some ways to reframe *recall* questions as *revealing* questions.

Recall	Reveal
• Which number should be the denominator? • What does Frederick Douglass say black people want (and don't want)? • What are the characteristics of fungi?	• Why do you know that's the denominator? • Why does Douglass say suffrage can (and must) precede schooling? • How do you know mosses aren't fungi?

These checks for understanding ought to occur not days or weeks after initial learning, of course, but immediately—within minutes. An analysis of more than 4,000 studies concluded that checks for understanding and immediate guidance can effectively double the rate of student learning (Wiliam, 2007). Here are some tips for making the most of checks for understanding:

- **Check often.** Ideally, you should check for understanding during each "chunk" of learning. As noted earlier, those segments should be 5–10 minutes long, so you'll likely want to check for understanding five times or more in a single hour-long lesson.

- **Ask revealing questions.** Douglas Fisher and Nancy Frey (2011) have observed that many teacher questions are often of the "guess what's in the teacher's head" variety (p. 61), asking for simple recall and recognition. Such questions serve a purpose: they provide a dipstick of sorts as to whether students are absorbing facts correctly and understanding what is important. Yet they do little to help us determine whether students are making sense of their learning. Do they see connections? Do they understand the *why* and *how* behind the *what*? Our questions should, accordingly, probe for this level of understanding.

- **Probe for mistakes and misconceptions.** It's also important to consider in advance the common mistakes students make or misconceptions they have about learning. For example, if you anticipate some students may misperceive seasons being the result of Earth "wobbling" on its axis, you can ask questions that reveal this and thus disabuse students of this misconception.

- **Stop talking and start listening.** On average, teachers talk about 70–80 percent of the time during class (Hattie, 2012). Yet the less teachers talk, the more students learn—and the more teachers learn about what their students are thinking and learning. "Chunking" lessons into 5- to 10-minute segments can help restore this balance by letting students talk more as they process information, interact with one another, and share their thinking. One simple way to listen to what students are learning is to ask them to engage in retelling—that is, asking them to summarize in their own words what they understand about what they've learned.

- **Engage all students.** Often, a handful of students do most of the talking in a classroom, while many never say a word. A study of 1,245 students in secondary science classrooms (Jones, 1990), for example, found that just 15 percent of students dominated the discussions, averaging 16 interactions

Try This: Numbered Heads Together

One proven approach for engaging all students in processing their learning—and checking their understanding of learning—is called *numbered heads together*. Students number off in groups of four and work together to formulate a response to a teacher's question, after which the teacher selects a number and asks students with that number to respond. This approach has been found to virtually eliminate student failure on subsequent content tests (Maheady et al., 1991).

per class, compared to 4 for their remaining classmates. Meanwhile, fully 29 percent of students said nothing whatsoever in class. To check the understanding of all students, it's important to replace undirected questions posed to the entire class with directed questions thoughtfully directed to individual students (Walsh & Sattes, 2005).

- **Review assignments for learning gaps.** Homework, quizzes, and writing assignments all offer a valuable window into student learning. As you review, grade, and record, you can check for understanding by looking for error patterns. Are several students failing to grasp the same concept or making similar mistakes? In particular, open-ended writing assignments that ask students to share their thinking are a good way to check for understanding and surface areas where reteaching may be needed (Fisher & Frey, 2011).

Provide Formative Feedback

Without feedback from teachers, practice assignments can become busywork, doing little to improve student performance. Although this may sound obvious, it's not uncommon to see classrooms where other students grade homework and pass it to the teacher, who then logs a score in the grade book and returns the assignment with little, if any, feedback. Without feedback, homework and other practice assignments can become an exercise in futility for students if they don't know what to do differently next time or where to focus their practice efforts. Hence, it's critical to couple practice with feedback—especially nonevaluative, formative feedback that helps students reflect on their progress and improve their performance.

As many studies show, feedback is one of the most powerful tools at your disposal. McREL researchers (Beesley & Apthorp, 2010), for example, found that giving feedback to students translates into an effect size equivalent to a leap of 28 percentile points on achievement tests over students who do not receive feedback. In his synthesis of research on several hundred education practices, Hattie (2009) found that giving students feedback ranked among the most powerful, prompting him to conclude that students need "dollops of feedback" (p. 238).

However, like many practices, not all feedback is good feedback. Indeed, despite the large overall effect size for feedback, fully one-third of studies on feedback examined in two seminal meta-analyses of research found negative effects for feedback on learning (Shute, 2008). With this in mind, here are some tips for ensuring your feedback supports rather than hinders student learning:

- **Ensure feedback is specific and actionable.** Basically, students should be able to do something with the feedback you give them; it should help them reflect on their learning and point them toward specific steps they can take to move closer to mastery (e.g., "Your essay tells your readers 'sleep is important'—how might you *show* that to them?"). In general, students benefit most from feedback given during or immediately after practice sessions with an important caveat: students need to think about their learning while practicing. For example, giving them the correct answer after each item on a test diminishes performance by letting their brains power down into low-effort mode instead of retrieving prior learning or thinking through a problem (Kulik & Kulik, 1998).
- **Keep feedback nonevaluative.** Several studies have found that when teachers' responses are highly evaluative or judgmental (e.g., "Right!" or "Wrong!"), low-performing students tend to shut down, avoiding interactions with the teacher for fear of embarrassment (Kelly & Turner, 2009). Feedback needs to come across in a way that doesn't sound judgmental but, rather, helpful, showing them how to improve their performance. This small adjustment in teachers' talk, in fact, often has a significant, positive effect on student motivation and engagement.
- **Keep feedback noncontrolling.** Similarly, students are more apt to take feedback well when it doesn't smack of trying to compel or coerce their behavior. A team of researchers led by Edward Deci (Deci et al., 1999) observed that even positive feedback from teachers can undermine student motivation if it comes across as coercing them to comply with a teacher's wishes (e.g., "You should keep up the good work"). Thus, when providing feedback, it's helpful to avoid words of obligation (e.g., *should,*

ought, need to) and replace them with observations and suggestions. For example, instead of saying, "I think you should . . . ," you might say things like, "Next time, you might try . . ." or "Where do you think you maybe got off track in solving that equation?"

- **Provide feedback that helps students think about their learning.** Perhaps most important, rather than coming right out and telling students what do to or how to correct a process, effective feedback helps students think about their learning—reflecting on their own misunderstandings or the missteps they may have taken. For example, instead of offering a correction or explicit guidance, your feedback should help them retrieve and apply prior learning (e.g., "Do you remember what to do if the digits in the right-hand column add up to more than 9?" "Remember, *venir* is an irregular verb, so how will you conjugate it?").

Interleave and Space Independent Practice

After guiding students' initial practice to ensure they have a solid understanding of the learning and/or know the right steps to follow, they'll likely still need some more repetitions to develop fluency with the skill and commit the new learning to memory—something they can do through less guided, independent practice. At this point, cognitive science points us to what may seem like a counterintuitive approach for both you and your students. Instead of practicing only one type of problem, rehashing the same knowledge, or rehearsing just one skill in a single session, it's best to mix up your practice—practicing the new type of problem, knowledge, or skill along with previously learned skills.

For example, if you've shown students how to "carry the one" with multicolumn addition, instead of giving them 20 problems that all require this process (e.g., 35 + 47), you might also mix in simpler problems (34 + 44) that don't require it. As you move on to new computations, you'll continue to sprinkle in multicolumn addition that requires carrying the one to solve correctly. Similarly, if you're teaching students irregular verb conjugations, you'll provide them with a mix of regular and irregular verbs to conjugate.

Such interleaved or mixed practice sessions should be provided as spaced practice sessions. Instead of asking students to work problems of the same type in one practice session never to be seen again before springing a test on them, you'll want to intentionally build into your unit design repeated exposures to, and practice with, new material. You might follow this general rule of thumb (drawn from Ebbinghaus's research): recap new learning after 20 minutes, 1 hour, 1 day, 2 days, 1 week, and 1 month.

Brace yourself, though. Your students may be confused. They may accuse of you trying to trick them. They may complain that you're "messing them up" by keeping them from mastering the new skill quickly in a single practice session dedicated to that skill. On this last point, they may be partly right. As noted earlier, massed practice does lead to fast learning—but also fast *forgetting*. Interleaving and spaced practice, meanwhile, can sometimes lead to weaker initial gains in proficiency but will ensure stronger gains later. So stick with it—your students will thank you later.

It's also worth noting that spaced practice opportunities can take many forms, including simple "retrieval" practice—that is, simply encouraging students to recall prior learning on ungraded pop quizzes, responses to classroom questions (e.g., "Close your notebooks, and on a blank sheet of paper, draw a picture of chloroplasts, their parts, and the molecular reactions going on inside them"), or cooperative learning activities that ask them to recall and quiz one another on what they've learned. The purpose here isn't to surprise, panic, or punish students but simply to boost their retention.

There's no need to grade these retrieval practice opportunities. If you fear students won't take retrieval practice seriously if you don't grade pop quizzes and the like, share with them the power of racking their brains to enhance their memories—that searching their minds for memories will keep them from fading and thus improve their performance when it really matters. Ideally, you want to help students see the power of retrieval practice so they begin to use it on their own, quizzing themselves and attempting to reproduce what they've learned in their own words.

Bear in mind that retrieval practice can be short and spontaneous. The sidebar provides some examples of retrieval practice exercises you can give students. As you'll see, none of these exercises takes much time, and many can be worked into other activities, such as "bell-ringer" exercises at the beginning of class. For example, as students sit down at their desks, you might give them a test or quiz from a prior unit to see how much they recall. You'll find that the more you engage students in regular retrieval practice, the more they'll come to expect it and anticipate the questions you'll ask them (and begin asking themselves those same questions).

Try This: Retrieval Practice

Retrieval practice simply asks students to rack their brains for prior learning, so activities using it needn't be complicated, lengthy, or graded. Here are some examples:

- **Pop quiz.** After a reading assignment or at-home practice session or during a classroom discussion, engage students in spontaneous (and individual) recall of key concepts to prompt them to search their memories for what they've learned.
- **Blast-from-the-past quiz.** Give students a previous quiz or section from a prior exam.
- **Partner quiz.** Have students write questions about the current lesson and pass them to one another to answer.
- **Brainstorm quiz.** Ask students to close their textbooks and, without looking at their notes, write a list of three to five key ideas they've just learned.
- **Give-one-get-one quiz.** Have students list two key ideas they've learned and then, in a limited time period (e.g., 90 seconds), move around the room giving one idea and receiving one idea from classmates until everyone builds a list of five to seven key ideas.
- **Exit quiz.** At the end of a lesson, give students a short quiz, which they score and give to you as an "exit ticket" when they leave the room.

Teach Students How to Practice

What's perhaps most striking about these strategies is how few students use them. For example, when 177 students at a prestigious university were asked to share their most common studying strategies, 83.6 percent reported "rereading notes or textbook" and 54.8 percent identified this as their go-to strategy; meanwhile, just 10.7 percent said they regularly engaged in self-testing, and only 1.1 percent listed it as their top strategy (Karpicke, Butler, & Roediger, 2009).

In theory, encouraging students to approach practice sessions focusing on skills or learning they have yet to master might sound like a simple matter of telling students to size up their learning and drill down on the most challenging areas (e.g., the multiplication tables they don't yet have down pat or the Spanish conjugations that bedevil them). In reality, though, many students overestimate what they know and underestimate how much they have yet to learn; thus, they tend to stop studying before they develop a true mastery of new learning. One reason for this is that when students first learn something, it may be present in their short-term memory, so they assume they've learned it (Nelson & Leonesio, 1988). However, when they try to recall that same bit of information from long-term memory 20 minutes or a day later, they're apt to find that it's vanished.

Moreover, students may believe—falsely—that they don't have any "bugs" in their knowledge. In fact, low-performing students tend to have the least accurate perceptions of their own abilities. In one study (Kruger & Dunning, 1999), students performing in the bottom quartile on tests of grammar, logic, and humor perceived themselves to be at the 60th percentile or higher, whereas performers in the top quartile put themselves in the 70th and 75th percentile, when they were actually, on average, at the 87th percentile. Low-performing students also tend to predict they will perform better on upcoming exams than they actually do yet demonstrate less certainty about their own predictions (Miller & Geraci, 2011). In short, students may struggle to engage in deliberate practice because they are unable to accurately size up their learning—or have a "fixed mindset" (Dweck, 2000) about learning that makes them fear they'll look or feel dumb if they admit to what they have yet to learn.

As a first step, explain to students the importance of deliberate practice (or, better yet, engage them in generating their own descriptions of effective practice). During this conversation, you can help them understand the power of identifying areas where they still stumble and engaging in concerted efforts to work through their rough patches. You might even share with them the Japanese concept of *kaizen* in which "every defect is a treasure" because it provides an opportunity to improve.

Next, you can encourage them to use retrieval practice as a means to identify these "treasures." For example, you can show students how to isolate and focus on the gap with a few quick repetitions (e.g., 8 × 7 = 56; 8 × 7 = 56; 8 × 7 = 56) or a mnemonic (e.g., ROYGBIV for the colors of the spectrum) and short-interval spaced practice, coming back to the new learning after a few minutes, an hour, or a day.

Although some of these practice strategies may seem obvious to you, that's probably because you mastered them yourself at some point in your academic career. Yet for many students, these simple practices remain a mystery. By giving them these simple "hacks" for learning, you can boost not only their performance but also their perception of themselves.

The Big Idea: Repeat Learning to Get It to Stick

As it turns out, our brains do an amazing job forgetting most of what we've learned. The so-called forgetting curve suggests we purge 90 percent of what we learn within 30 days—with most of that forgetting happening within the first few hours (Medina, 2008). That means without well-designed opportunities to practice and reflect on their learning, students will forget most of what they learn in your classroom today before they hit their beds tonight. And what they don't forget during their waking hours, their brains are prone to finish off as they sleep, purging anything that seems useless—especially any new learning they never revisited or retrieved after it was splattered across their working memories.

The good news, though, is that new studies are finding that while our sleeping brains erase many new memories—scientists have observed synapses shrinking during sleep—they've also observed larger synapses partially, if not entirely, spared from pruning (Cirelli & Tononi, 2017). In short, our brains appear to recognize the neural networks we spent time building and reinforcing during the day are important and, in a sense, "marked" for storage; thus, the neural janitor that works its way across our brains at night, clearing away our useless memories, "sweeps" around these new memories so they remain available to us.

By purging most new memories and sparing only a few, sleep may help us reduce the "noise" of the many useless memories that accumulate in our brains during the day and thus increase the signal-to-noise ratio in our brains, allowing us to consolidate memories into learning. As neuroscientist Giulio Tononi puts it, sleep allows us to "forget in a smart way" (Zimmer, 2017, p. D5), yet it all depends on repeating new learning sufficiently during the day so our brains mark it as worth sparing at night.

In light of all this repetition, some students may find this phase of learning to feel long on drudgery and short on curiosity; they may feel the "fun" stuff—the joy of discovery and grappling with cool ideas—is behind them, and now they must endure the tedium of rehashing stuff they've already learned, like chewing on a piece of gum long after it's lost its flavor.

Is that true? Do students need to set curiosity aside to practice new learning? Only if they do it wrong. If all they do is mindlessly repeat what they've learned, practice is likely quite tedious . . . but that's not how to practice. The best kind of practice is *deliberate*, which requires students to ask questions (i.e., stay curious) and reflect on their progress as they practice.

For example, as they seek to master a skill, they need to stay curious to reflect on what's working (e.g., "When I 'place' my voice in my nose, I can really sing that high note!") and what's not (e.g., "I think I understand the law of cosines, but I'm not getting these problems right. What am I missing?"). Similarly, when students struggle to retain a new concept, idea, or vocabulary term, they likely need to pause a moment to reflect on their learning process, asking themselves how else they can commit the concept to memory (e.g., a visual, a personal connection, a mnemonic). Perhaps most important, they may need to reengage their curiosity to fully wrap their minds around the concept, asking themselves, "Do I really understand this? Can I explain it to someone else? Do I know why it's important? Can I connect it to other ideas?"

All this boils down to the key idea of this chapter: to get learning to stick, students must return to their new learning, thinking and rethinking about it within minutes of learning it—and multiple times thereafter. Yet even with this deliberate practice and reflection, the journey is far from over.

Every night as students sleep, the neural janitor in their brains will return, looking for more useless information to purge. If learning stops too soon—if all we do is ask students to retrieve knowledge on, say, an exam—their new learning will remain fragmented, fragile, and quick to fade because their brain's night janitor won't deem it worthy of retaining.

In the next chapter, we'll explore how to ensure this doesn't happen by helping students take learning to its final phase—one that engages them in extending and applying what they've learned so they can connect it with other ideas, knowledge, and skills in increasingly complex neural networks that reflect deep and lasting learning.

7

Extend and Apply

On December 3, 2016, chess master Timur Gareyev (who later graced the cover of *Chess Life* playing chess while skydiving) traveled to Las Vegas to perform his tour de force: simultaneously playing 48 opponents while blindfolded. As he pedaled on an exercise bike, his opponents called their moves out to him. Holding an image of all 48 boards in his mind, he called his countermoves back to them. Twenty-three hours, 50 miles, and 1,400 moves later, Gareyev set the world record, completing 48 simultaneous, blindfolded matches—winning 35, taking a draw in 7, and losing 6 (Barden, 2017).

At first blush, one might assume Gareyev has superhuman powers of memory, yet when cognitive scientists ran a battery of tests on him, they found nothing remarkable about him. "We didn't find anything other than playing chess that he seems to be supremely gifted at," said one of the researchers (Sample, 2016). So how did Gareyev do it? One trick was a technique called a "memory palace." He created 48 rooms in his mind and gave each chess move a name—for example, he labeled a D4 opening "Princess Diana" and pictured Princess Diana in that room. If, on the next round of play, his opponent moved the adjacent pawn (an E4 move, code-named "Elvis"), he'd picture Elvis joining Diana in the room (Lubin, 2017).

Another, likely more important, memory aid was something all chess masters appear to do. Researchers found that grandmasters could memorize the exact location of four times as many pieces on a board as novice players (Chase & Simon, 1973). At first blush, that might suggest having a better memory is critical to their expertise, yet a simple twist in the study showed that expertise was the key to better memory. When researchers placed chess pieces randomly on the board (i.e., not as the result of gameplay), experts could memorize the position of no more pieces than novices. In short, they didn't have better memories but, rather, the ability (developed over thousands of hours of practice) to see patterns of moves.

This phenomenon points us toward what needs to happen in the final stage of learning for it to stick. First, we must engage in deep consolidation—building on prior learning and arranging what we've been learning into larger, coherent patterns. Second, we must develop multiple retrieval hooks for new learning so we can readily conjure it up and apply it.

Cognitive scientists sometimes refer to this process of seeing a problem for what it is (e.g., "Looks like that cut is infected . . .") and conjuring up the right script in our minds to solve it (e.g., ". . . better get some antibiotic ointment") as a *schema* or a mental model. In popular vernacular, we often call it good old-fashioned know-how. Arguably, "know-how" is the main goal of learning. After all, our aim is precisely to help students connect knowledge and skills together to better understand the world around them and take informed action that creates positive outcomes for themselves and others.

As we'll see in this chapter, developing mental models requires doing more than simply parroting learning back on a test; it requires extending and applying our learning, often by engaging in critical and creative thinking about what we're learning and applying it in new situations to solve problems. In many ways, this final phase of the learning journey also brings us right back to where we started—helping students become interested in new learning. With this final phase of learning, we help them stay interested in their learning by finding meaning and purpose in it.

If we lop off this final stage, we're apt to leave students with experiences that feel like a futile exercise of taking tests, jumping through hoops, and "playing the game" of schooling, disconnected from real life, meaning, and purpose. As a result, students may fail to consolidate what they've learned in meaningful ways or generate sufficient "hooks" to retrieve it later.

In this chapter, we'll build on what we previously learned about memory storage and retrieval to explore more deeply how our brains convert information into useful knowledge and skills we can retrieve later when we need it. You'll also learn how to give your students opportunities to extend and apply their learning so they can develop mental models and retrieval hooks that serve them for a lifetime.

The Science of Deep Learning

Let's return for a moment to an idea we touched on in the last chapter—namely, that there's a big difference in the processes required to store and retrieve memories. As I discovered on my return to my college alma mater after a long absence, many erstwhile "forgotten" memories came rushing back to me. As it turns out, they'd been there all along, but my hooks for retrieving them had withered away until I exposed myself again to the sights, sounds, and smells I'd associated with those memories many years earlier.

No doubt, you've had similar experiences—storing something in your memory that you couldn't retrieve until some sort of triggering event or cue shook it loose. Conversely, you've no doubt held something strongly in your memory but only for a little while. For example, the last time you went to the store, you likely held in your memory where you parked your car for the 30 or so minutes you were shopping. A week later, though, if someone were to ask you to testify in a court of law where you parked your car, you'd likely struggle to recall it.

All this happens because, as Elizabeth and Robert Bjork (1992) describe in their "New Theory of Disuse," storing memories requires a different mental process than retrieving them. *Storing* memories typically requires repetition of new learning—and sometimes a third factor: strong emotions, positive or negative. For example, you'd probably remember, without rehearsal or retrieval practice, where you parked your car a week ago if another driver dented the fender or, conversely, if an anonymous, kind soul left you a $100 bill under your wiper blade.

Retrieving memories, on the other hand, requires developing multiple pathways to the memory, creating several hooks for our brains to extract it later. In the previous chapter, we mostly explored how practice and repetition build storage strength. In this chapter, we'll explore the other side of the coin: how to help students build retrieval strength by developing multiple mental connections to their new learning, thereby creating many hooks so they can extract what they've learned when they need it.

Relating New Learning to Ourselves

Let's start with a simple yet powerful principle of memory retrieval: we're more apt to recall new learning when we make a personal connection to it (Sousa, 2011). Researchers figured this out years ago when they asked students to study lists of words with different "depth of processing" strategies. For example, some students considered the meaning of the words while others considered the words' phonemics or structure. Not surprisingly, the students who contemplated the meaning of words retrieved more of them later. Retrieval was even stronger for a third group of students—those who related the words to *themselves* (e.g., "Does the word describe you?") (Rogers et al., 1977, as cited in Symons & Johnson, 1997).

Over the years, researchers found similar positive effects for this so-called self-reference effect in a variety of other learning tasks, age groups, and subject areas—so much so that a meta-analysis of 129 of these studies concluded that relating new learning to ourselves and our experiences has a powerful, often additive, effect on recall (Symons & Johnson, 1997). In one study, researchers asked three groups of college students to study a chapter on child development using different methods. One group asked themselves self-referencing questions while reading; another used the more elaborate SQ4R method (survey, question, read, reflect, recite, review); and a third selected the study strategy of their choice (most chose highlighting and rereading) (Hartlep & Forsyth, 2000). The researchers tested the students immediately after the study session and then again two weeks later. On both exams, students who connected the reading to their own personal experiences outperformed the other groups—far better than the control group and even better than students using the more elaborate SQ4R method, which suggests the key element of that entire method may well be reflection, during which it's likely students connect what they're reading to their own experiences.

Why should connecting what we're learning to ourselves and our own experiences be such a powerful learning strategy? The short answer is researchers aren't exactly sure, though they suspect that when we connect new learning to personal experiences, we are, in effect, fusing it with existing neural networks, which increases the storage strength of the new learning. At the same time, because we've connected the new learning to personal experiences, it's likely that we're more apt to encounter cues in our environment that remind us of what we've learned, thereby increasing retrieval strength.

Imagine, for example, if you were to only focus on the semantic meaning of a word such as *petulant*, repeating the definition over and over in your mind ("irritable or sulking in a childish way"). You might struggle to find a place (i.e., an existing neutral network) to store that word in your mind. If, on the other hand, you relate the word to someone you know, like a friend who pouts when she doesn't get her way, you're more apt to put that word in a mental bucket, perhaps one labeled "annoying friend traits." On top of that, you now have a retrieval cue that's apt to be reinforced. For example, if your friend gets surly when the groups decides to go to a different restaurant than her choice, you'll be reminded of the word.

A final point to make here is that self-reference needn't be narrowly (or narcissistically) focused on oneself to have a positive effect (Symons & Johnson, 1997). We appear to create equally powerful organizers for storing and retrieving new learning whether we relate it directly to ourselves or to others, including the world around us. In fact, studies suggest altruistically minded students, in particular, may benefit more from linking learning not to themselves as individuals but to what it means for helping those around them.

Asking Ourselves Deeper Questions

Another learning strategy that's been shown to increase retrieval strength of new learning is called elaborative rehearsal or elaborative inquiry. Basically, it takes retrieval practice a step further by encouraging students to elaborate on their learning by asking themselves more complex *how*, *why*, and *what if* questions about what they're learning (McDaniel & Donnelly, 1996). For example, students might consider *why* leaves turn colors in the autumn, *how* an air conditioning system works, or *what* would've happened *if* the United States hadn't joined the Allies in World War II.

Laboratory studies (Pressley, McDaniel, Turnure, Wood, & Ahmad, 1987) have demonstrated the power of elaborative interrogation by, for example, presenting three groups of college students with different sentences about a man's action. One group read a list of simple sentences (e.g., "A hungry man got into a car"). A second group read similar sentences with an elaboration, such as "A hungry man got into a car to go to restaurant." And a third group—the elaborative inquiry group—read the same simple sentences as the first group but were also asked to offer an explanation: "Why did the man do that?"

After reading 24 such sentences, the students were given a pop quiz to see if they could recall the behavior of each man (e.g., "What did the hungry man do?"). As it turns out, students who engaged in elaborative inquiry had much higher recall of each man's behavior, correctly answering, on average, 65 percent of the questions versus 15 and 24 percent, respectively, for groups that had read the simple and more elaborate sentences.

Cognitive scientists (Dunlosky, Rawson, Marsh, Nathan, & Willingham, 2013) believe that elaborative interrogation solidifies learning in our minds by helping us connect new learning with prior knowledge and, more precisely, existing *mental models* (discussed later in this chapter). Basically, the process unfolds like this: If we're prompted to consider "How exactly does warm air rise?" we might think, "Well, I know warm air expands and becomes less dense, just like how air is less dense than water. So maybe it's like an air bubble rising in a glass of water." At this point, we're fusing new learning with previously constructed mental models (e.g., expansion, density, water bubbles, gravity) and can thus "piggyback" our new learning onto retrieval hooks we've already attached to those mental models. Now, instead of just having one or two retrieval hooks, we have many, making it easier for our brains to grab onto and extract the new learning.

Studies across many age groups, ability levels, and content areas have demonstrated the power of students asking themselves deeper questions (Chi, de Leeuw, Chiu, & LaVancher, 1994; Schworm & Renkl, 2006; Scruggs, Mastropieri, & Sullivan, 1994; Smith, Halliday, & Austin, 2010; Wong, Lawson, & Keeves, 2002; Wood & Hewitt, 1993). It's worth noting, though, that as with the self-reference effect, asking elaborative questions really only works when learners have already focused on, and made sense of, new learning and are ready to strengthen their storage and retrieval of their new learning (Woloshyn, Pressley, & Schneider, 1992). For example, asking students to explain why an airfoil wing helps planes fly won't help them encode the information more deeply if they don't already understand the underlying principles of, say, air pressure.

Explaining Ourselves

Elaborative inquiry has been shown to support the encoding and recall of *declarative knowing*—facts, concepts, and ideas (Dunlosky et al., 2013). What about *procedural knowledge*—skills, procedures, and processes? As it turns out, a similar process called self-explanation supports encoding of skills-based learning. Basically, self-explanation entails talking aloud through the steps of a process we're taking and the choices we're making as we follow those steps. For example, when solving a math problem, we might ask students questions like, "Why do you need to cross multiply here?" or "Why does it work to multiply length and width to calculate the area of a rectangle?"

British researcher Dianne Berry (1983) tested this idea by asking students to solve logical puzzles using jars of jam and record labels by either talking through them aloud or solving them silently. As students engaged with these tasks, Berry asked one group of students to explain their reasoning aloud as they solved the problems and another group to explain their reasoning *after* solving the puzzles; a third group engaged in the tasks without verbalizing. After the first two tasks, all three groups showed strong command of the rules, solving more than

90 percent of the puzzles correctly on the second trial. Yet in the third phase of the experiment, when Berry tested students to see how well they could transfer their learning—in particular, the rules of logic underlying these tasks—to a similar yet slightly more abstract task using cards, the experiment took an interesting turn.

Only the students in the self-explanation group had the same success as before; they solved 90 percent of the problems correctly, successfully transferring learning from the concrete (jars and records) task to the abstract (cards) one. However, students in the after-the-fact explanation and no-explanation groups stumbled badly, answering correctly just 68 and 27 percent of the time, respectively. Consider that for a moment. Despite having already solved what was basically the same problem, students who hadn't talked through the logic of solving it failed to connect the dots, or transfer learning, between the concrete and abstract tasks.

Why should this be? We don't know for sure, but it's likely the think-alouds helped students think about their learning (connecting visual and verbal processing) and, in so doing, spot the underlying pattern in the tasks from which they could extract a general rule that helped them transfer their learning to a novel challenge—in this case, the card puzzle (Berry, 1983). Perhaps most surprising, even when Berry came right out and told students that the card puzzle was basically the same as the jars of jam and record label puzzles (i.e., telling them that "although the materials are different, the tasks are logically identical"), those who hadn't talked through the puzzles were no more able to transfer their learning to the new task.

These results suggest two things. First, it's one thing to know *what* and *how* to do something and quite another to understand *why* it works—that is, the underlying logic or guiding principles of the problems we're solving. Second, it would appear that[the best way to understand the logic of, or patterns, in what we're learning is to talk through *why* we're doing *what* we're doing.]For whatever reason, this process of thinking aloud seems to be instrumental in helping us better connect what, how, when, and why together into larger, coherent patterns.

Creating Mental Models

Researchers often call these coherent patterns *schema* or *mental models*. They've also found that mental models appear to be fundamental building blocks of deep learning. Without mental models, it's difficult, if not impossible, to consolidate learning in a way that helps us make sense of the world around us or solve complex problems.

Imagine, for example, you wake up one Saturday morning and decide that after years of kids, dogs, foot traffic, and spilled drinks, it's time to invest in a new living room carpet. Before going to the carpet store, though, you decide to see if you can afford new carpet by figuring out how much carpet to buy and what it will cost. As a first step, you measure the walls in your living room, which is in something of an *L* shape. After doing this, you create a rough sketch of the room, like the one in Figure 7.1, labeling the length of each wall in feet. You see from a local ad that carpet costs about $75–$100 per square yard. At this point, you find yourself starting down the barrel of a real-life word problem.

Let's consider what happens in your brain as you work to solve this problem. First, you must retrieve some declarative knowledge to size up the kind of problem you're going to solve— calculating the area of a polygon. Next, you must retrieve a process for solving the problem: *length* × *width* = *area*. You recognize, though, that you're not dealing with a simple rectangle here. Now you retrieve more procedural knowledge to help you figure out how to calculate the area: break the shape into two smaller rectangles. You continue in this fashion— toggling back and forth between declarative and procedural knowledge—to sort

Figure 7.1
Living Room Dimensions

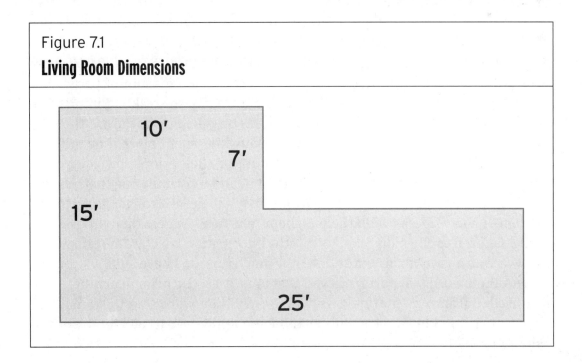

through the conversion from square yards to square feet and finally to calculate the price. By drawing on different types of knowledge, you solve the problem and, to your dismay, realize one room of new carpet will cost upward of $3,000 before add-ons like carpet pads, installation, and the like. A quick look at your bank account leads to a change of plans: you'll spend the weekend rearranging furniture to cover the stains in your carpet.

As it turns out, this sort of interweaving of declarative and procedural knowledge is not only key to solving complex problems; it's what distinguishes experts from novices in a variety of fields and endeavors—from medicine (Lesgold et al., 1988) to mathematics (Silver, 1979) to architecture (Akin, 1980) to firefighting (Klein, 1998). Unlike novices, experts can more readily cluster multiple data points into recognizable patterns to better understand problems and then summon procedural knowledge to solve them (Nokes, Schunn, & Chi, 2010).

Basically, experts engage in a process that goes something like this: when confronted with a problem, they (1) categorize a problem; (2) construct a mental representation of it; (3) search for appropriate problem-solving strategies; (4) retrieve and apply those strategies; (5) evaluate the effectiveness of the problem-solving strategies used; (6) repeat steps 1–4 if they don't arrive at a solution; and (7) if arriving at a correct answer, store that solution and process for later use (Newell & Simon, 1972).

By contrast, when researchers (Brand-Gruwel, Wopereis, & Vermetten, 2005) tracked how novices (first-year college students) approached a complex task—in this case, researching and writing a 400-word essay on whether it's best to follow printed expiration dates or trust our senses when consuming perishable foods—they observed that novices tended to plunge into the task, spinning their wheels by poring over useless information and struggling to categorize the new information. Experts (doctoral students), meanwhile, spent more time initially sizing up and categorizing the problem, reflecting on their prior knowledge, evaluating new information as they encountered it, and reformulating their theses based on new information. Most important, they showed a stronger grasp of the problem-solving process, which helped them continually assess their progress by asking themselves questions like, "Is this the information I need? Am I still working toward an answer to my question? How much time do I have left?"

In other words, experts showed a strong grasp of prior learning, having encoded it into mental models, which they then were able to transfer to a new situation; that is, they could extend and apply prior learning to solve a complex problem.

Thinking Critically About Our Mental Models

As noted earlier, when we retrieve prior learning, we effectively make it pliable again so we can connect it to other ideas and experiences. What that also means is that every time we retrieve and apply prior learning in the form of mental models, we not only make our mental models more robust but also have the opportunity to revise our mental models if we find they fail to help us solve a problem or fully comprehend the world around us.

No doubt you do this all the time in your classroom. For example, when a lesson that once worked splendidly doesn't fly with your current students, you realize your existing mental model (e.g., that kids really dig *Lord of the Flies* or your cherished stock market simulation unit) may no longer be true. Herein lies the key to expertise: not getting stuck on a single interpretation of events but, rather, continuing to reexamine and *refine* our mental models—engaging in a process we might call critical thinking.

What this suggests is that extending and applying learning—giving students opportunities to develop, retrieve, and refine their mental models—is perhaps the best (if not only) way to help them develop critical thinking skills. Although critical thinking remains ill-defined, researchers generally tend to regard it as a complex set of dispositions and skills, including valuing inquisitiveness and other points of view, applying logical reasoning to create and support arguments, and examining our own beliefs and being open to changing them in light of new, contradictory data (Abrami et al., 2015; Bangert-Drowns & Bankert, 1990).

Perhaps most important, we really only engage in critical thinking once we have deep knowledge in a particular area or field. In other words, we must know a good deal about something before we can think critically about it. As cognitive scientist Daniel Willingham (2007) has observed, critical thinking is not a skill in the usual sense of the word—something we can learn in one field and easily transfer to another. Rather, we must learn and employ the principles of scientific thinking with science knowledge, textual analysis with literature, historical thinking in social studies, quantitative reasoning in mathematics, and so on.

Ultimately, we develop critical thinking skills by learning new content and seeing how it applies to the real world, which allows us to examine our own thinking and refine our mental models if we find they are inadequate or inaccurate. While reading the previous chapter, for example, you may have found yourself refining your own mental models about practice when learning about interleaving, spaced practice, and location-dependent retrieval. That's great.

Being comfortable with and knowing when to change your mind is the hallmark of expertise.

Going "Meta" (Thinking About Our Thinking)

A final principle of deep learning is one that in many ways encapsulates all the other principles. It's also something you've likely learned to do as you've grown as a professional educator and learned to reflect on your own practice, employing what researchers call metacognitive thinking about your teaching. In simple terms, metacognition is thinking about thinking; it's the voice in our heads that prompts us to pause, reflect, and redirect when we note a gap or something breaking down in our learning. This running commentary in our heads helps us connect new and prior knowledge, refine mental models, and generate new questions to guide our learning.

As it turns out, the ability to engage in metacognitive thinking—or to "go meta"—is also essential for students and something we help them develop as they extend and apply new learning. It's worth noting, in fact, the original McREL research study (Marzano, 1998) that formed the basis of *Classroom Instruction That Works* (and many of the classroom toolkit strategies included in this book) sought to examine the effects of learning strategies across three key broad mental processes: (1) the *self system* (which guides whether we see learning as valuable and believe we can be successful in it), (2) the *cognitive system* (which processes new knowledge and skills), and (3) the *metacognitive system* (which monitors learning in relation to our desired outcomes). Across all the studies examined in the meta-analysis, those that reflected metacognitive strategies—in particular, helping students clarify goals for learning and reflect on the strategies they're using to achieve their goals—had the largest effect sizes.

What this suggests is that engaging in metacognitive thinking is a key to deep learning. Basically, to learn anything deeply, we need a voice in our head that guides us to pause and process when we don't understand it. We need a voice that helps us connect what we're learning to our personal experiences. We need a running commentary that helps us summarize our learning and extract guiding abstract principles from what we're learning that we can apply in other settings. And we benefit from having an internal monologue that helps us connect dots, spot larger patterns, and develop mental models. Conversely, failing to engage in metacognitive thinking while learning often leaves us with a mishmash of learning that's disconnected, faulty, or void of meaning—tidbits of knowledge that are apt to fade quickly from memory because they have little meaning, relevance, or utility for us.

Extend and Apply: A Classroom Toolkit

Now that students have focused on new learning, made sense of it, and practiced it, you're finally ready to help them engage in a challenging learning activity that will help them extend and apply their new knowledge and skills by connecting it to themselves, developing and refining their mental models, and thinking critically about what they're learning. In so doing, they will create more complex and robust memory storage and retrieval, making their learning "stickier." Moreover, by employing the following strategies to help them "go meta" with their learning, the real magic of learning can occur—namely, students taking ownership of what they're learning and becoming increasingly thoughtful, reflective, and curious learners.

Provide Challenging Learning Tasks

A useful starting point for helping students extend and apply their learning is engaging them in learning tasks that are in their "Goldilocks" zone of challenge—that is, tasks that are neither too difficult nor too easy but "just right" for them. Research, in fact, shows students are most motivated to learn when engaged in learning they believe they can achieve yet challenges them. So, with this in mind, here are some guiding principles for creating learning tasks that provide a "just right" level of challenge for students:

- **Engage students in thinking about big ideas.** As noted earlier, students are more apt to retain learning when they consolidate it into big ideas, themes, and mental models. As standards and curriculum documents often fail to identify these big ideas for students, you may need to extract them on your own (or with colleagues) by looking for them within the content of your learning. Some ways big ideas reveal themselves include recurring themes (e.g., individual freedoms versus social cohesion), conceptual frameworks or models (e.g., the water cycle), paradoxes (e.g., smaller nations often prevail over larger ones), insights and wisdom (e.g., our desires often bring unhappiness), and guiding principles (e.g., supply and demand drive prices).

- **Provide students with personally relevant learning choices.** Studies show we can increase student motivation by giving them meaningful choices (Patall et al., 2008). Moreover, as we've seen with the self-reference effect, students engage in deeper encoding and retrieval of learning when they can align what they're learning with their personal interests. It's worth noting here, though, that choices needn't be exhaustive or entirely student directed (e.g., "Study any topic you like!"). In fact, too many choices can diminish motivation by causing students to expend too much mental energy on choosing what to learn (or worrying they might make the "wrong" choice). As researchers who examined numerous studies of the impact of learning choices on motivation put it, "too much of a good thing may not be very good at all" (Patall et al., 2008, p. 298). What's often better is a handful of structured choices (e.g., teacher-selected topics to study or texts to read).
- **Engage students in cognitively demanding work.** Students only learn what they think about. Too often, learning tasks leave students expending mental energy on activities ancillary to what we want them to learn. It's not uncommon to see school walls bedecked with student artifacts that reflect inordinate amounts of time and mental energy focused on cutting, pasting, coloring, or formatting—instead of thinking deeply about science, history, literature, or foreign languages. So, as you create learning tasks for students, consider what you want them to think about as they engage in those tasks. What questions do you want them to consider? What ideas do you want them to explore? In what ways do you want them to make their thinking visible?
- **Support independent learning.** During this final phase of the journey, you're turning the process of learning over to students, in keeping with the "I do, we do, you do" gradual release of responsibility model. As you make this shift, though, recall that novice learners, in particular, often don't have the same skills as more expert learners to monitor and guide their own learning. Left to their own devices, they may spin their wheels—for example, wordsmithing a written report that requires more substantial reorganization. As students begin to engage in more independent learning, you'll likely need to provide them with checklists, exemplars, and timelines to follow—and plan for multiple check-ins to see how they're doing.

Support Inquiry-Based Learning

The heart of any challenging learning task should be a driving question—an inquiry that taps into students' curiosity through an investigation, opportunity to apply new learning, analyze a complex system, or challenge or synthesize what they've learned into a creative activity. McREL's own research on effective instructional strategies, published in two editions of *Classroom Instruction That Works*, identified a handful of effective instructional strategies that engage students in extending and applying learning grouped under the category "generating and testing hypotheses." Although testing hypotheses is the heart of the scientific method, it might be more accurate to categorize this collection of strategies more broadly as strategies for inquiry-based learning—that is, asking and engaging students in pursuing compelling, difficult-to-answer questions that defy a simple, straightforward answer. These research-based strategies, which have all been linked to higher levels of student learning, are as follows:

- **Problem solving** involves identifying and describing constraints that prevent people from achieving real-life agreed-upon goals and then finding ways to overcome them. Typically, it starts with identifying a shared goal (e.g., there's too much litter on campus) and describing the conditions that arc creating the problem and/or barriers to resolving it (e.g., people like to eat lunch outdoors when it's warm outside; there aren't enough trash cans outdoors). Next, students work (independently or collaboratively) to develop solutions to change the underlying conditions or overcome the barriers to the problem (e.g., we could start an antilitter campaign and talk to school administrators about putting more trash cans and recycling bins outdoors) and offer a hypothesis about which solution is most likely to work. Students then test the solution, either in reality or through a simulation (e.g., we'll launch a "be proud of your school" anti-littering campaign for two weeks and count pieces of litter in the school yard to see if it decreases). After collecting and analyzing data, students explain whether their hypothesis was correct and whether they need to test another hypothesis or develop and test a different solution (e.g., the schoolyard has less litter, but the trash bins are overflowing now, so perhaps we need both solutions).

- **Experimental inquiry** engages students in scientific thinking about all manner of problems, inviting them to generate and test explanations of observed phenomena. It starts with inviting students to observe various phenomena and describe what they see (e.g., certain objects float while others sink). Next, with facilitation, if necessary, students develop specific theories or rules to what they've observed (e.g., lightweight items float and heavy ones sink; items that displace water float). Based on their explanations, students generate hypotheses to predict what might happen in a new a situation (e.g., the pumice stone will sink because it's a rock; the pumice stone will float because it has tiny pockets of air in it) and then set up an experiment or activity to test the hypothesis (e.g., place the stone in a jar of water). Afterward, they explain the results of the experiment or activity (e.g., the stone floated) and determine if the hypothesis is correct or if additional experiments are needed to generate and test a new hypothesis.

- **Systems analysis** engages students in the critical thinking exercise of examining the parts of a system and how they interact. The process begins with students explaining the purpose of a system, its parts, and the function of each part (e.g., the economic components of the housing market consist of supply, demand, and access to financial capital). Next, students describe how the parts of the system interact with one another (e.g., as demand increases, prices rise, especially if buyers have access to capital). Once students understand how the system works, they develop hypotheses about how altering one part of the system might affect its other elements (e.g., looser lending rules allow more buyers to take out loans). Finally, students test the hypothesis through an experiment, simulation, or use of historical data (e.g., as more buyers access loans, home prices climb beyond the point of affordability, creating a housing bubble).

- **Investigation** invites students to identify and resolve issues about which there is confusion, contradiction, or controversy. This process begins with students describing the concept, historical event, or hypothetical future scenario to predict. For example, students might engage in an investigation to discover why Ice Age megafauna disappeared. Next, they identify what is already known or agreed upon (e.g., megafauna such as mastodons disappeared as global temperatures began fluctuating wildly and humans entered their habitat). Once the facts are laid out, students develop a hypothesis based on what's known about the situation (e.g., humans killed the megafauna in an "overkill" scenario). Students engage in gathering and analyzing evidence to determine if the hypothetical scenario is plausible (e.g., archaeologists have found mastodon bones in the campsites of Ice Age humans).

As noted earlier, students can engage in these sorts of inquiries in a variety of content areas beyond science to speculate about the relationship between two variables (e.g., Did the Huns cause the fall of the Roman empire? Were Romeo and Juliet's tragic deaths the result of fate or bad decisions?).

McREL's meta-analysis of 11 scientific studies (Beesley & Apthorp, 2011) found that engaging students in these sorts of inquiry-based learning opportunities not only enhanced their understanding of lesson concepts (Hsu, 2008; Tarhan & Acar, 2007; Tarhan, Ayar-Kayali, Urek, & Acar, 2008) but also supported their ability to transfer knowledge to new situations (Marx et al., 2004; Rivet & Krajcik, 2004; Ward & Lee, 2004)—an effect size of 0.61 when compared with more teacher-led instructional activities, such as lectures or sequenced activities. Basically, when we pose open-ended questions to students and give them the mental tools to answer them (but not the answers), we help them think through (often aloud or in writing) what they're learning so they can transfer their learning to new situations.

Make Student Thinking Visible

As noted earlier, studies show that one of the best ways to help students transfer prior learning is to encourage them to make their thinking visible (to themselves and others) both as they process new learning and when they transfer it to new situations. Here are some ways to do this:

- **Employ elaborative interrogation.** After students demonstrate an initial grasp of a concept or new idea, encourage them to reflect on and stretch their thinking by considering questions such as "How exactly does that work? Why should that be true? What if it weren't true?" (McDaniel & Donnelly, 1996). For example, you might ask students to consider *why* it works to cross-multiply fractions, *how exactly* releasing compressed air cools a room, or *what if* Hannibal had made it across the Alps with his elephants and army?

- **Engage in self-explanation.** Encourage students to think aloud while learning new procedural knowledge. For example, when correcting sentence punctuation, ask them why a comma is needed to separate a compound sentence. Similarly, when solving a complex mathematics problem, ask them to articulate *why* a particular computation is the right one (e.g., "Why is the original number the denominator when calculating increasing or decreasing percentages?"). If they're analyzing whether a political ad contains fact or opinion, ask them to explain their reasoning (e.g., "You said a term like *wasteful spending* is an opinion—why?").

- **Ask the "Golden Question."** Glen Pearsall (2018) refers to this simple question—*What makes you say that?*—as the "Golden Question." While simple, it's also powerful because it helps students share their reasoning and lets other students hear what their peers are thinking, which, in turn, helps every student reflect on and clarify their own thinking. It's also versatile; it's a simple question that can be used in any subject or grade level.

Teach Critical Thinking

Providing students with opportunities to extend and apply their learning also helps them develop critical thinking skills. In fact, according to several studies, reflecting and drawing on prior learning may be the only way to develop critical thinking skills. Two big ideas emerge from studies of how to help students develop critical thinking:

- **Teach students how to think critically.** A meta-analysis of critical thinking approaches (Bangert-Drowns & Bankert, 1990) concluded that critical thinking doesn't develop through osmosis; simply exposing students to literature, science, history, or logical proofs does little to develop their critical thinking skills. Instead, we must actually *teach* students to think critically and give them opportunities to practice it. A study of students in low-performing high schools (Marin & Halpern, 2010) placed students in three different groups: one received explicit instruction in critical thinking (learning how to develop arguments, identify stereotypes and rigid mental models, and predict the long-term consequences of decisions); a second group took an introduction to psychology workshop with critical thinking "embedded' into its lessons; and a control group proceeded with regular coursework. When all three groups were retested three weeks later on their critical thinking abilities, the explicit instruction group demonstrated significant gains in critical thinking, whereas the embedded instruction and control groups showed no gains.

- **Teach critical thinking within content knowledge.** Another meta-analysis identified three essential elements for developing students' critical thinking: (1) classroom discussion, (2) complex problem solving, and (3) mentoring (Abrami et al., 2015). One study in the meta-analysis—an examination of a "historical thinking" pedagogy in a high school American history course (Pellegrino, 2007)—illustrates these findings. With teacher mentoring, students engaged in an independent inquiry to develop and present their own views on a historical period and the developments that shaped it, drawing on multiple sources to support their explanations. Simultaneously, classroom discussions encouraged them to understand differing views of history. With all three elements in place—dialogue, complex problems, and mentorship—students demonstrated significant gains in critical thinking ($d = 1.13$).

Try This: *Because*

A simple way to help students develop critical thinking is one suggested by Silver and colleagues (2018): ask students to support their responses with the word *because* (e.g., "I know this is the right answer/best interpretation/ most plausible explanation/strongest argument *because . . .*"). It's a simple yet powerful word—a concentrated drop of critical thinking that compels students to extend their thinking about their learning.

Sharpen Thinking via Writing

Numerous studies have linked the act of writing and deep learning. That's likely because turning what we're learning into writing forces us to wrangle what's often a flurry of thoughts swirling around our minds, pack them together into coherent ideas, turn those ideas into words, and, ultimately, stack those ideas to together into a narrative, argument, or explanation of the world. As writer Flannery O'Connor put it, "I write because I don't know what I think until I read what I say."

Here's what we know from research about the power of writing to support deep learning. A meta-analysis of 93 studies (Graham & Hebert, 2010) found engaging students in structured writing had significant effects on reading comprehension—likely because it makes their thinking visible and engages them in arranging new learning into coherent patterns. These studies, in fact, show that inviting students to write about what they're reading had a greater effect on comprehension than many other strategies, such as reciprocal teaching. These same studies also show that engaging students in writing had a particularly pronounced effect for low-ability students, especially when they also received direct instruction on how to arrange their thoughts into coherent writing.

Research also makes a strong case for using writing to help students extend, apply, and synthesize their learning in all content areas. For example, in schools where science teachers require students to engage in regular writing and note taking, 79 percent of students score at proficient levels versus just 25 percent of students in science classrooms where writing and note taking remains rare (Schmoker, 2011).

Although only a few studies to date have examined the link between critical thinking and writing (e.g., Quitadamo & Kurtz, 2007), a small but in-depth study provides some evidence to suggest properly designed writing assignments support critical thinking (Langer & Applebee, 1987). For the study, researchers monitored a group of six students trained in think-alouds to hear what students were thinking about while reading social studies texts using three different methods: note taking, answering study questions, and writing an analytical essay. When answering study questions, students engaged in fragmented, low-level recognition and recall. When the students took notes, their learning became more coherent, yet they still failed to connect it to bigger ideas and themes. Only when writing the essay did they engage in more complex, critical thinking, synthesizing, hypothesizing, and evaluating what they were learning.

Finally, it's worth noting that according to a meta-analysis of research on the effects of writing on student achievement (Bangert-Drowns, Hurley, & Wilkinson, 2004), writing assignments needn't necessarily be inordinately time-consuming to be effective—they simply need to engage students in making their thinking visible by putting their thoughts into words. Here are a few writing exercises that are effective for helping students of all ages extend and apply their learning in a variety of subject areas:

- **Summary narrative.** A summary narrative is a straightforward writing assignment in which "students retell events or a process from an imagined personal perspective" (Urquhart & Frazee, 2011, p. 57). For example, students might reconstruct the story of Hannibal marching on Rome from Hannibal's perspective. Such assignments are engaging for students and help them make meaning of what they're reading.
- **Essay writing.** Longer (e.g., five-paragraph) essays help students arrange and integrate their thinking. Essay assignments should, of course, clearly align with success criteria and challenge students not simply to regurgitate facts and ideas but to think more deeply about their learning, inviting them to explain *why* a particular event occurred in history or *how* a process works, or to engage in *what if* thinking (e.g., "What if Columbus had landed in Brazil instead of the Caribbean?").
- **Argumentative essays from two points of view.** Students identify a controversial topic—for example, should assault weapons be banned? They research and write two essays—one from each point of view. Both essays are scored on the same rubric, which challenges students to think deeply about a topic, including perspectives different from their own.

Anchor Learning to Performance Assessments

We all know the old maxim "What we measure is what we get." Too often, though, assessments tend to measure only low-level (e.g., recall and recognition) declarative knowledge or chunks of procedural knowledge (e.g., solving a particular type of math or science problem). If we want students to extend and apply their learning in deeper, more meaningful ways, we also need to assess their learning in more powerful ways that guide them to demonstrate their ability to weave declarative and procedural knowledge together in order to solve complex problems and engage in higher-order thinking about what they're learning.

Consider for a moment the process of obtaining a driver's license. Typically, it includes three important components: a traditional multiple-choice test covering basic facts, a period of learning and driving practice, and a behind-the-wheel performance test. Knowing the multiple-choice test is coming, a driver candidate digs into the licensing manual, memorizing information on stopping distances, the meanings of signs, and other rules of the road. Nevertheless, such "book learning" alone doesn't render the aspiring driver safe behind the wheel. Thus, we ensure they can put their foundational knowledge to work by extending and applying what they've learned by getting behind the wheel and engaging in practice driving under the watchful eyes of a parent or driving instructor. Achieving mastery takes time, practice, and plenty of formative feedback to help driver candidates prepare for the final performance assessment: showing an examiner they can apply their (declarative) knowledge and (procedural) skills to safely operate a car on a driving test.

Performance assessment works in a similar way in classrooms, requiring students to show they can effectively extend and apply their knowledge and skills by creating a product, presentation, or demonstration (i.e., a performance) (Pecheone & Kahl, 2014). Performance assessments call on students to extend their learning, connect it with prior learning, think creatively and/or critically about it, and apply it in a real-world setting. Research shows that performance assessments provide better measures of student knowledge and skills—not to mention improve student engagement and motivation, increase teacher buy-in and collaboration, improve the quality of instruction (Darling-Hammond & Wood, 2008), and support critical thinking (Faxon-Mills, Hamilton, Rudnick, & Stecher, 2013).

So what does it look like in a classroom? As it turns out, it looks a lot like a learning opportunity that follows the phases of learning we've described in this book, including these steps:

Step 1: Identify the critical declarative and procedural knowledge necessary to master success criteria and encourage students to commit to learning challenging goals.

Step 2: Give students multiple opportunities to focus on, make sense of, practice, and research their knowledge.

Step 3: Regularly check student understanding of the knowledge through retrieval practice (e.g., ungraded quizzes), short writing assignments, and class discussion.

Step 4: Engage students in an end-of-unit challenging, project-based learning task that requires them to extend and apply their learning.

Step 5: Provide all students with an independent learning activity through which they demonstrate mastery of the new learning.

Step 6: Give all students a rubric so they can self-evaluate and revise their learning artifact accordingly.

Step 7: Provide all students with a summative evaluation (e.g., a grade and feedback) for the performance assessment—and, ideally, opportunities to revise their work based on the feedback.

The following sidebar offers a further example of what this process might look like in a classroom. Done well, performance assessments not only support deeper learning but also unleash student engagement and motivation.

Try This: A Curriculum-Embedded Performance Assessment

Here's a brief example of what it might look like to embed performance assessments into classroom curriculum. A full example would include content standards, success criteria, scoring rubrics, and sample student work.

Heat Transfer

Activity 1: Students individually or in small groups research methods of heat transfer. They discuss what they have learned about conduction, convection, and radiation (*student-guided learning*).

Activity 2: Teachers check student understanding of methods of heat transfer via ungraded quizzes, interviews, or class discussion (*formative assessment evidence gathering, feedback,* and *adjustment*).

Activity 3: In small groups, students design and conduct an experiment to determine which of two fabrics better protects against the winter cold. Materials required include tin coffee cans of different sizes (with lids), two different fabrics (e.g., plastic and wool), fasteners, thermometers (thermal probes), timers, and hot water (*performance activity*).

Activity 4: Students individually write up a formal lab report of their experiment (*graded summative product*).

Activity 5: Teachers, via questioning, lead a class discussion of how methods of heat transfer played a role in the design and implementation of the research (*formative assessment reflection and reinforcement*).

Activity 6: Students individually research how a home heating system works and write a paper describing a home heating system and how different methods of heat transfer are involved (*graded summative product*).

The Big Idea: Helping Students Develop Richer Mental Models

Ultimately, providing students with these sorts of opportunities to extend and apply their learning can help them develop what's at the heart of deep learning: mental models. As we've seen, such mental models are also at the heart of another important cognitive process: critical thinking. In classic chicken-or-egg fashion, mental models and critical thinking appear to be inextricably linked. We need mental models to engage in critical thinking, which in turn helps us shape and refine our mental models.

Simply stated, to think critically, we need *something* to think about. So let's take a moment to dispel a myth that sometimes floats around education and goes something like this: In today's information age, there's no need for students to learn facts because they can simply Google them. Instead (so the thinking goes), we should focus on helping students develop critical thinking skills. Like most myths, there's a kernel of truth to this argument, yet in the end, it really doesn't stand up to closer scrutiny.

Cognitive science shows us that, in reality, critical thinkers tend to accrue and consolidate a tremendous amount of knowledge—in the form of mental models, which they continue to refine and revise as they encounter new information and solve new problems. This brings us to another, closely related myth we ought to dispense with, too. This one says students learn best when they're forced to wrestle with complex challenges—that they must "discover" for themselves solutions to challenges. Here, again, research suggests it's not exactly true.

After conducting a series of studies on the power of complex problems to support deep learning, Australian researcher John Sweller (1988) came to an important conclusion—and caveat—for educators. Simply challenging students with complex problems won't do much to help them develop complex problem-solving skills. In fact, it might backfire.

Why? Because novice students lack mental models for categorizing problems and conjuring methods to solve them. As a result, if we throw them into the deep end unaided, they are apt to expend a great deal of mental bandwidth (what Sweller called "cognitive load"), toggling back and forth between figuring out how to solve a problem and actually trying to solve it. As a result, even if they ultimately arrive (laboriously) at a correct answer, they won't actually develop any mental models for future use because the processes they engaged in to get the right answer and to develop an understanding of how they arrived there (i.e., mental models) appear to be, as Sweller put it, "two largely unrelated and even incompatible processes" (p. 283).

In other words, students should develop some basic mental models prior to engaging in challenging learning tasks and inquiry, during which they can refine mental models yet not necessarily develop them from scratch. Consider, for example, a systems analysis task that engages students in considering how altering one economic, social, or political condition in the American colonies prior to the Revolutionary War might have changed the outcome of that conflict. Engaging in this activity would require students to have many preexisting mental models of trans-Atlantic trade patterns, philosophies of government, religious beliefs, and the motivation of various colonial groups. If we were to plunge students into the middle of this exercise, though, without first helping them develop these mental models, we'd just create frustration and weak learning, which likely explains why "discovery learning" activities produce mixed results. For example, an analysis of studies of "instruction using minimal guidance" (Kirschner et al., 2006) found mostly dismal results, especially for lower-aptitude students, who benefit from "stronger," more teacher-directed instruction in which they are shown, for example, the steps required to complete an algebra problem and are provided with models for solving the problem.

It's also worth reiterating that although developing mental models and critical thinking is a sophisticated process, it's not the privileged domain of highly gifted or more advanced students. All students, even young ones, develop mental models—from the mechanics of rainfall to the arc of a story narrative to skip counting on number lines. Even these basic concepts represent forms of mental models. Over time, as we help them accrue, consolidate, and refine more mental models, students develop the building blocks of expertise and, along the way, discover that deep down, everyone has an expert inside them waiting to come out.

8

Where to Go from Here

There you have it—a complete model for learning. Please take it as it's intended, though—not as a rigid, step-by-step formula for your classroom but, rather, as something more akin to a blueprint for learning and a springboard to help you develop your own expertise and mental models as an educator.

Going "Meta" to Build Your Expertise

As noted in the last chapter, having well-developed mental models is often what distinguishes experts from novices. As you absorb the contents of this book into your own practice, you'll hopefully feel increasingly like a chess grandmaster who can quickly size up a game board, recognize patterns in it, and think strategically about your next moves. Perhaps most important, applying this model in your classroom will help you "go meta" about your own practice, considering not just *what* you're doing but *how* it's affecting student learning and *why* you're doing it. In so doing, you'll become more adept at doing what experts do: connect declarative knowledge (i.e., mental models) with procedural knowledge (i.e., skillful execution of mental scripts, sequences, or steps).

Consider, for example, what distinguishes a veteran quarterback from a rookie. As the veteran approaches the line, he spots movement in the opposing team's defense. Drawing on what he knows about defensive schemes (i.e., his declarative knowledge), he immediately sees what's happening: several defenders are planning to charge across the line in a "blitz." Just as quickly, he conjures mental scripts (i.e., his procedural knowledge) to consider alternative courses of action and then calls out an audible, telling his team to run a different play—a quick pass to the sidelines to evade the rushing defenders. A rookie quarterback, meanwhile, may observe the same thing but lack the declarative knowledge to understand what he's seeing or the procedural knowledge to know how to adjust the play. So he runs the original play as called from the sidelines; the defense rushes him, and he gets tackled behind the line for a loss.

Arguably, a classroom has just as many moving parts as a football game. As a result, novice teachers often do something similar to rookie quarterbacks. They develop a playbook (a lesson plan) that often focuses mostly on what they'll do as a teacher and pay less attention to what students will be doing—and what ought to be happening in students' minds as they engage in the lesson.

By applying the model described in this book in your classroom, you're starting with what you want to see happen at each step along the way for student learning—not simply following a playbook for your teaching. In so doing, you'll be better prepared to diagnose what's going well and what's going poorly in your classroom and to make real-time adjustments, calling a few "audibles" now and then to get learning back on track. Sports metaphors aside, what goes on in a classroom is far more important than a football game, so it's important we develop expertise in our classrooms because our students are counting on us.

Using the Learning Model to Reflect on Your Teaching

As we've noted earlier, what distinguishes an expert from a novice—and a profession from a job—is that experts and professionals use deep knowledge of their practice (in the form of mental models) to diagnose and solve problems. As you incorporate each element of the learning model into your profession, take notice of the changes it brings about for students.

For example, as you become more intentional and proficient with the "become interested" phase of learning, you should see students becoming more engaged in their lessons. Similarly, as you help students focus on "committing to learning" by giving them a "what's in it for me" and helping them develop and internalize success criteria, you should notice they are better able to sustain their focus and concentration on learning, especially if you regularly remind them of their success criteria. As you do these things, pause and ask yourself what differences you observe. Doing so will allow you to further refine your practices and mental models.

Using the Model to Diagnose Student Learning

Another key benefit of using a learning model to guide the design and delivery of student learning experiences is that when you notice students are struggling to grasp ideas or develop skills, you can better diagnose where learning may be breaking down. For example, you might ask these questions:

- Were students disengaged with the learning? If so, you can reexamine what you did (and might do better) to help them become interested in or committed to learning.
- Do students appear to understand some things well and others poorly? If so, you might consider what you did (and might do differently) to help them focus on new learning or make sense of their learning. For example, you might make learning more visual or give them more time to process learning, connecting new knowledge to prior knowledge or clustering it into bigger ideas.
- Do students struggle to apply new skills? If so, you might consider what different practice or feedback opportunities they need to refine their skills.
- Does their knowledge remain superficial? That is, do they appear to understand new learning yet struggle to transfer it to new situations or apply critical thinking skills (e.g., analyzing, evaluating, synthesizing, creating) to it? If so, you may need to consider how to help them better extend and apply learning.

Using a Learning Model to Support Professionalism and Collegiality

A final benefit of applying this model to your classroom and considering the science of learning behind it is that doing so can help you engage in professional dialogue, collaboration, and peer coaching with your colleagues. Indeed, a defining characteristic of any profession is that professionals don't operate in a vacuum or go it alone. Rather, they engage in intensive learning experiences through which they develop a shared vocabulary and understanding of their field so they can work together. A doctor in an emergency room doesn't say, for example, "Hand me the sharp pointy thing so I can slice into this guy's ticker." Instead, health professionals use precise language of medical instruments and the human body along with shared mental models about, for example, the human circulatory system, to work together as professionals to solve complex problems.

Here are few ways a learning model can support professionalism and collegiality in your school or school system:

- **Engage in professional dialogue.** Perhaps the biggest benefit of having a shared model of learning is it enables you to engage in professional dialogue with your colleagues. Much like doctors who use a common vocabulary and understanding of medicine to evaluate patients' symptoms, a common vocabulary for learning makes it possible to consult with colleagues about what's happening when students struggle to learn.

- **Share and codevelop units and lessons.** Equally important, a common model of learning makes it easier and more efficient to codevelop and share lesson and unit plans. Similar to how the Android and Apple operating systems provide a common platform for software developers to create and share millions of apps for smartphones, this tiny bit of standardization—a common model for units and lessons—can help you and your colleagues share lesson and unit plans. When everyone in your school or district uses the same language and understanding about how lessons should flow into larger (extend-and-apply) learning opportunities for students, it's easier to share lessons.

    That means that while a common model of learning supports some routinization of teaching and learning, it needn't diminish teacher creativity or professionalism. Far from it. If anything, a shared model of learning—especially one built on the science of learning and student curiosity—can serve as a springboard for creativity and ingenuity, letting teachers create and share units and lessons that engage students in deep learning across classroom, schools, and school systems.

- **Engage in peer coaching on what matters most.** Research shows that the best way to deeply embed professional practices in classrooms is not through bird-dogging or browbeating teachers but, rather, engaging everyone in peer coaching. Indeed, only when the introduction of a new theory, models for better practice, and opportunities to practice new learning are supported with peer-to-peer coaching do teachers appear to transfer new practices into their classrooms (Joyce & Showers, 2002).

    However, to ensure peer-to-peer coaching is effective and doesn't turn into vague, wishy-washy conversations, participants need a shared understanding of what good teaching looks like. This is where it's helpful to have a shared model of learning—one that provides you and your colleagues with a common vocabulary and mental models for designing and delivering effective learning experiences for students and the same starting point for expanding and refining your repertoire of teaching strategies.

Frequently Asked Questions

As you and your colleagues begin to work together to assimilate this knowledge into your own mental models and professional practice, you'll likely have some questions. In an effort to anticipate some of those queries, here are some responses to questions teachers often ask as they begin to apply this learning model in their classrooms.

Do I really need to help students become interested with *every* lesson?

Only if you *want* them interested in every lesson! In short, this question pretty much answers itself. That said, in practice, you'll likely find that you may need to give students different "hooks" for becoming interested in a larger unit than individual lessons. If you've given students a compelling reason to be interested in a unit (e.g., a mystery prompt such as "How could an empire—Rome—that once spanned most of the known world could fall into a decay and ruin?"), you can draw students back to that larger question as you introduce individual lessons in the unit (e.g., "Some historians believe Atilla the Hun caused Rome to fall. Today, we'll explore arguments for and against this position so you can come to your own conclusion about whether the brutal Atilla—who died in suspicious circumstances *before* Rome fell—caused the mighty empire to collapse").

Should students commit to learning goals or objectives?

Yes! That is, they should have both. Larger, long-term learning goals (e.g., "I want to learn why Rome fell so I can see whether the same thing might happen to the West") will likely connect with units, whereas shorter-term objectives/ success criteria will connect with lessons (e.g., "I'll be explaining the arguments for and against whether Atilla led to the demise of Rome").

Does every lesson require an "extend and apply" phase?

Not exactly. You needn't help students extend and apply learning for each lesson but, rather, frame opportunities for them to extend and apply learning over the course of a unit. You might think of it this way: lessons provide building blocks of basic knowledge and skills that students extend and apply to engage in a challenging learning task or inquiry at the end (or during the course) of a unit. For example, students might learn several theories for the fall of Rome, which they integrate as a final inquiry to develop and defend their own arguments for the fall of Rome.

Does the learning model align with essential questions?

Yes, absolutely. In fact, providing or helping students develop guiding questions for a unit can be a powerful way to activate their curiosity (e.g. "I want to know why Rome fell and if the same conditions that caused the fall of Rome might be present in the Western world today"). Each lesson, in turn, may have its own, smaller guiding question (e.g., "We'll learn arguments historians make for and against Atilla the Hun being a culprit in the fall of Rome so that we can determine whether we want to include it in our own historical argument").

The learning model seems sequential. Is learning really so linear?

Nope. It's not. In fact, it's a more iterative and messy process than a strictly superficial interpretation of this model (e.g., Phase 3 always follows Phase 2) might suggest. We often focus on and make sense of new learning, for example, in a cyclical manner; we learn something new, make sense of it, then add another new bit of learning to what we've just learned. Similarly, practice and reflection can lead to new learning as we recognize gaps in our understanding or skills we need to refine. And as we gain new insights, we may become more interested in and recommitted to learning new knowledge and skills.

It's also OK to intentionally deliver learning "out of sequence." For example, you may find it works to jump right into a science experiment to demonstrate a concept—that is, focus students on new learning—then go back to sparking students' curiosity and commitment to learn the concept you've just demonstrated by asking them what they think happened. That said, even though the phases of learning needn't always occur in the exact sequence presented here, all six phases remain essential. Indeed, it's difficult to imagine deep learning occurring if any are ignored or omitted.

Consider, for example, a scene I observed shortly before writing this paragraph as I walked through Hyde Park in Sydney, Australia. Some young men were practicing tricks on skateboards. I have no idea the exact sequence of their learning but could surmise they had engaged in all six phases of the model. Given their persistence in practicing tricks they were far from mastering (sorry, lads), they'd clearly become interested in and committed to learning. It was also clear that at some point, they'd focused on new learning—likely through watching other skaters flip their boards in midair and land on them. I also heard them talking to one another about their efforts to land the trick, engaging, as it were, in a form of cooperative learning to make sense of their learning. Their current phase of learning—practicing and reflecting—was itself a form of extending and applying prior knowledge of riding skateboards and making small jumps to land a more difficult trick. This learning likely didn't unfold in a tidy, linear fashion but in messier, iterative phases.

Should I teach this model to my students?

Absolutely! In fact, some teachers displayed icons for each phase of the learning model to show students where they are in the process—pointing, for example, to the "commit to learning" icon as students set learning goals. Helping students understand how their own brains work can help them become more meta-cognitive about their own learning and make course corrections if, for example, they realize something doesn't make sense to them. By sharing the process with students, you can also invite their feedback on your instructional choices. For example, you might ask them questions such as "Did our cooperative learning activity help you to make sense of learning? Did our final project—our extend-and-apply activity—stretch your thinking in new and different ways?"

Bringing Curiosity and Joy to Teaching and Learning

Of all the wonders of the universe, one of the most amazing may well be the three-pound lump of gray matter inside your skull: the human brain. Our minds can filter, process, and assimilate vast amounts of data every second of the day and turn it into learning—often with little or no formal schooling. I found myself thinking about that as I observed the teens on their skateboards in the park in Sydney. Their tireless efforts to learn new skateboarding tricks were entirely self-motivated. At least, I didn't see any teachers giving them homework or telling them they'd be tested and graded on their ability to land new tricks the following Monday. Unprompted and untested, the young men had joyfully surrendered a Friday evening in the park to engage in—that's right—learning.

The Brain in Its Natural State: A Voracious Learner

That's the beauty of the human brain—it's an incredible learning machine, especially when we set our minds to learning something. In fact, that's the whole point of this book. The learning model described here attempts to harness and reflect learning in its natural state—when it occurs through self-motivated inquiry into learning; when we find ourselves lost in the flow of learning, losing track of time even, as we immerse ourselves in pursuing curiosity and learning skills that we find personally relevant and meaningful.

All too often, though, classrooms subject students to something quite different: sitting through lessons that alternately underwhelm their brains—subjecting them to dry, uninteresting, or vapid busywork—and overwhelm their brains, barraging them with disconnected bits of information and leaving them with little time to process what they've learned before subjecting them to massed practice sessions that encourage fast forgetting of new learning and truncating the entire process so they never consolidate any learning to long-term memory.

In short, the typical classroom often creates unnatural conditions for learning—conditions that run counter to what we know about learning. As cognitive scientist John Medina puts it, "If you wanted to create an education environment that was directly opposed to what the brain was good at doing, you probably would design something like a classroom" (2008, p. 5).

Teaching with Curiosity in Mind

This book aims to correct that situation by providing you with a model for learning that's designed to help you tap into students' natural aptitude and appetite for learning, including what science has shown to be one of the most powerful drivers for learning: curiosity. As noted earlier, curiosity primes our brains for learning and taps into something that's at the core of our being. As human beings, we are naturally curious—we're born to learn.

Consider that point for a moment. Before children ever enter school or formal education or a classroom of any kind, they learn hundreds, if not thousands, of words. They learn motor skills like walking, running, and climbing. How do they do all that? Because they're curious. Because they want to learn new things and find it enjoyable. Indeed, science shows that every time we close a knowledge gap—that is, satisfy our curiosity—our brains are flooded with dopamine—the same "reward molecule" we receive when we win a prize, eat something sweet, or have a first kiss. In short, learning, when unfettered and motivated by curiosity, is rewarding, fun, and, well, addictive.

You've no doubt seen young children become so absorbed in their own curiosity—for example, discovering that when they pull one tissue from a box another pops up in its place—that they become so oblivious to their surroundings that they're unaware you're watching them from the doorway as they empty the box into a pile tissues in front of them. You've likely also seen young children's incessant need to ask questions, attempting to make sense of their world—asking one why question after another. That's the joy of curiosity.

You've also seen them practice something, over and over again, without prompting. They stand up. Walk a few steps. Fall down. Then they start the process all over again, developing muscle memory. Soon, they take their new learning and try it out in a novel setting, extending and applying it to climb stairs, to jump up and down, to hop on one foot, to run, to chase after pets, and to skip down the sidewalk. All the while, their brains are rewarding them for their learning, releasing chemicals like dopamine when they achieve their goals, close their knowledge gaps, and satisfy their curiosity.

Making Learning Easier and More Joyful in Your Classroom . . . and Your Professional Life

In sum, this learning model is an attempt to help us design learning opportunities for students that reflect how we naturally learn. Our job as teachers is merely to accelerate the natural process of learning, by inserting new, interesting, and important ideas and concepts that keep curiosity alive, so the process unfolds as naturally and seamlessly for an 18-year-old as it does for an 18-month-old. When we do this—design learning opportunities that reflect our students' brains' natural propensity for learning—the entire enterprise of learning gets easier and more joyful.

Hopefully, this book has done the same for you as a professional, helping you become interested in how the process of learning works and feeling inspired to commit to learning and apply these ideas to your own practice. You may have noticed that each chapter in this book was designed to help you focus on new learning and make sense of learning, connecting new ideas to your own prior learning and classroom experiences. Because real learning will only really happen as you practice and reflect on these concepts and strategies in your classroom, we've tried to provide you with practical examples and tools for your classroom. Perhaps most important, we hope you'll use this book as a springboard for digging deeper and asking your own questions about learning—and how it works for your students and in your own particular context. We hope you'll engage in your own inquiry-driven, curiosity-fueled professional learning and, in so doing, extend and apply this model—molding, sculpting, and adapting it to your own practice.

Making the Model Your Own

In closing, it's worth noting that while the learning model in this book is deeply rooted in research and the science of learning, *it is just a model*—an attempt to grasp an incredibly complex process called learning. In short, it's not intended to paint a definitive, precise picture of how learning happens for everyone in every situation.

After all, models—even complex scientific models—are just stories we tell to explain something before we fully understand it. Over time, as you apply and reflect on your use of this model in your own classrooms, you'll likely refine and adapt it into your own model for learning. That's as it should be. It's what experts do—develop and refine mental models.

Ideally, you'll see this book not as providing The Model to follow—a be-all and end-all of what it means to be a good teacher—but, rather, a companion on your professional journey, one that generates as many questions as it answers. Hopefully, this book has made you curious as a teacher and excited to continue your professional learning journey—sparking your curiosity, fanning the flames of your professional inquiry, and fueling your inner fire to keep exploring and learning something new every day about the amazing profession you've chosen to pursue—to be a changer of students' lives.

References

Aben, B., Stapert, S., & Blokland, A. (2012). About the distinction between working memory and short-term memory. *Frontiers in Psychology, 3,* 301.

Abrami, P. C., Bernard, R. M., Borokhovski, E., Waddington, D. I., Wade, C. A., & Persson, T. (2015). Strategies for teaching students to think critically: A meta-analysis. *Review of Educational Research, 85*(2), 275–314.

Akin, O. (1980). *Models of architectural knowledge.* London: Pion.

Anderson, J. R. (1995). *Learning and memory: An integrated approach.* New York: Wiley.

Assor, A., Kaplan, H., & Roth, G. (2002). Choice is good but relevance is excellent: Autonomy affecting teacher behaviors that predicts student engagement in learning. *British Journal of Educational Psychology, 72,* 261–278.

Baddeley, A. D., & Hitch, G. (1974). Working memory. In G. H. Bower (Ed.), *The psychology of learning and motivation: Advances in research and theory* (Vol. 8, pp. 47–89). New York: Academic Press.

Baddeley, A. D., & Logie, R. H. (1999). Working memory: The multiple-component model. In A. Miyake & P. Shah (Eds.), *Models of working memory: Mechanisms of active maintenance and executive control* (pp. 28–61). New York: Cambridge University Press.

Bailey, F., & Pransky, K. (2014). *Memory at work in the classroom: Strategies to help underachieving students.* Alexandria, VA: ASCD.

Bandura, A., & Schunk, D. H. (1981). Cultivating competence, self-efficacy, and intrinsic interest through proximal self-motivation. *Journal of Personality and Social Psychology, 41*(3), 586.

Bangert-Drowns, R. L., & Bankert, E. (1990, April). *Meta-analysis of effects of explicit instruction for critical thinking.* Paper presented at the annual meeting of the American Educational Research Association, Boston.

Bangert-Drowns, R., Hurley, M., & Wilkinson, B. (2004, Spring). The effects of school-based writing-to-learn interventions on academic achievement: A meta-analysis. *Review of Educational Research, 74*(1), 29–58.

Barden, L. (2017). Grandmaster plays 48 games at once, blindfolded while riding exercise bike. *The Guardian.* Retrieved from www.theguardian.com/sport/2017/feb/10/timor-gareyev-48-chess-games-blindfolded-riding-exercise-bike-leonard-barden

Baser, M. (2006). Fostering conceptual change by cognitive conflict based instruction on students' understanding of heat and temperature concepts. *Eurasia Journal of Mathematics, Science and Technology Education, 2*(2), 96–114.

Baser, M., & Geban, Ö. (2007). Effectiveness of conceptual change instruction on understanding of heat and temperature concepts. *Research in Science & Technology Education, 25*(1), 115–133.

Beesley, A. D., & Apthorp, H. S. (2010). *Classroom instruction that works: Research report* (2nd ed.). Denver, CO: Mid-continent Research for Education and Learning.

Beeson, S. A. (1996, September). The effect of writing after reading on college nursing students' factual knowledge and synthesis of knowledge. *Journal of Nursing Education, 35*(6), 258–263.

Berry, D. C. (1983). Metacognitive experience and transfer of logical reasoning. *Quarterly Journal of Experimental Psychology Section A, 35*(1), 39–49.

Bethell, C., Newacheck, P., Hawes, E., & Halfon, N. (2014). Adverse childhood experiences: Assessing the impact on health and school engagement and the mitigating role of resilience. *Health Affairs, 33*(12), 2106–2115.

Bjork, R. A., & Bjork, E. L. (1992). A new theory of disuse and an old theory of stimulus fluctuation. In A. F. Healy, S. M. Kosslyn, & R. M. Shiffrin (Eds.), *From learning processes to cognitive processes: Essays in honor of William K. Estes* (Vol. 2., pp. 35–67). Hillsdale, NJ: Erlbaum.

Bjork, E. L., & Bjork, R. A. (2011). Making things hard on yourself, but in a good way: Creating desirable difficulties to enhance learning. *Psychology and the Real World: Essays Illustrating Fundamental Contributions to Society, 2*, 59–68.

Bloom, B. S. (1956). *Taxonomy of educational objectives. Vol. 1: Cognitive domain.* New York: McKay.

Bloom, K. C., & Shuell, T. J. (1981). Effects of massed and distributed practice on the learning and retention of second-language vocabulary. *Journal of Educational Research, 74*(4), 245–248.

Boch, F., & Piolat, A. (2005). Note taking and learning: A summary of research. *The WAC Journal, 16*, 101–113.

Boring, E. G. (1957). *A history of experimental psychology* (2nd ed.). Englewood Cliffs, NJ: Prentice Hall.

BouJaoude, S., & Tamin, R. (1998, April 19–22). *Analogies, summaries, and question answering in middle school life science: Effect on achievement and perceptions of instructional value.* Paper presented at the annual meeting of the National Association for Research in Science Teaching, San Diego, CA (ERIC Document ED 420 503).

Brand-Gruwel, S., Wopereis, I., & Vermetten, Y. (2005). Information problem solving by experts and novices: Analysis of a complex cognitive skill. *Computers in Human Behavior, 21,* 487–508.

Bransford, J., Brown, A., & Cocking, R. (2000). *How people learn: Brain, mind, experience, and school* (Expanded ed.). Washington, DC: National Academy Press.

Bransford, J. D., & Johnson, M. K. (1972). Contextual prerequisites for understanding: Some investigations of comprehension and recall. *Journal of Verbal Learning and Verbal Behavior, 11*(6), 717–726.

Bremner, J. D. (2006). Traumatic stress: Effects on the brain. *Dialogues in Clinical Neuroscience, 8*(4), 445–461.

Bridgeland, J. M., DiIulio, J., & Morison, K. B. (2006). *The silent epidemic: Perspectives of high school dropouts.* Washington, DC: Civic Enterprises.

Broer, N., Aarnoutse, C., Kieviet, F., & van Leeuwe, J. (2002). The effects of instructing the structural aspects of text. *Educational Studies, 28*(3), 213–238.

Bronson, P., & Merryman, A. (2010, July 10). The creativity crisis. *Newsweek.* Retrieved from www.newsweek.com/2010/07/10/the-creativity-crisis.html

Brophy, J. (2004). *Motivating students to learn* (2nd ed.). Mahwah, NJ: Erlbaum.

Brown, P. C., Roediger, H. L., McDaniel, M. A. (2014). *Make it stick: The science of successful learning.* Cambridge, MA: Harvard University Press.

Busteed, B. (2013, January 7). The school cliff: Student engagement drops with each school year [blog post]. *Gallup Organization.* Retrieved from https://news.gallup.com/opinion/gallup/170525/school-cliff-student-engagement-drops-school-year.aspx

Calderon, V. J. (2017, June 8). How to keep kids excited about school [blog post]. *Gallup Organization.* Retrieved from https://news.gallup.com/opinion/gallup/211886/keep-kids-excited-school.aspx

Cerasoli, C. P., Nicklin, J. M., & Ford, M. T. (2014). Intrinsic motivation and extrinsic incentives jointly predict performance: A 40-year meta-analysis. *Psychological Bulletin, 140,* 980–1008.

Chase, W. G., & Simon, H. A. (1973). Perception in chess. *Cognitive Psychology, 4,* 55–81.

Chen, O., Castro-Alonso, J. C., Paas, F., & Sweller, J. (2018). Undesirable difficulty effects in the learning of high-element interactivity materials. *Frontiers in Psychology, 9*(1483), 1–7.

Chen, Z. (1999). Schema induction in children's analogical problem solving. *Journal of Educational Psychology, 91*(4), 703–715.

Chi, M. T. H., de Leeuw, N., Chiu, M.-H., & LaVancher, C. (1994). Eliciting self-explanations improves understanding. *Cognitive Science, 18,* 439–477.

Cialdini, R. B. (2005). What's the secret device for engaging student interest? Hint: The answer is in the title. *Journal of Social and Clinical Psychology, 24*(1), 22–29.

Cirelli, C., & Tononi, G. (2017, May). The sleeping brain. *Cerebrum.* Retrieved from www.ncbi.nlm.nih.gov/pmc/articles/PMC5501041

Coleman, J. S. (1966). *Equality of educational opportunity study.* Washington, DC: U.S. Department of Health, Education, and Welfare.

Cornelius-White, J. (2007). Learner-centered teacher-student relationships are effective: A meta-analysis. *Review of Educational Research, 77*(1), 113–143.

Cotton, K. (1998). *Classroom questioning.* Portland, OR: Education Northwest. Retrieved from https://educationnorthwest.org/sites/default/files/ClassroomQuestioning.pdf

Csikszentmihalyi, M., Rathunde, K. R., & Whalen, S. (1993). *Talented teenagers: A longitudinal study of their development.* New York: Cambridge University Press.

Curwin, R., Mendler, A., & Mendler, B. (2018). *Discipline with dignity: How to build responsibility, relationships, and respect in your classroom* (4th ed.). Alexandria, VA: ASCD.

Darling-Hammond, L., & Wood, G. (2008). *Assessment for the 21st century: Using performance assessments to measure student learning more effectively.* Washington, DC: Forum for Education and Democracy.

Davis, A. P. (2015, August 20). I survived my terrifying hour in a sensory-deprivation tank. *New York.* Retrieved from www.thecut.com/2015/08/i-survived-my-terrifying-hour-in-a-float-spa.html

Deakin, J. M., & Cobley, S. (2003). An examination of the practice environments in figure skating and volleyball: A search for deliberate practice. In J. Starkes & K. A. Ericsson (Eds.), *Expert performance in sports: Advances in research on sport expertise* (pp. 90–113). Champaign, IL: Human Kinetics.

Dean, C. B., Hubbell, E. R., Pitler, H., & Stone, B. (2012). *Classroom instruction that works* (2nd ed.). Alexandra, VA: ASCD.

Deci, E. L., Ryan, R. M., & Koestner, R. (1999). A meta-analytic review of experiments examining the effects of extrinsic rewards on intrinsic motivation. *Psychological Bulletin, 125*(6), 627–668.

Dunlosky, J., Rawson, K. A., Marsh, E. J., Nathan, M. J., & Willingham, D. T. (2013). Improving students' learning with effective learning techniques: Promising directions from cognitive and educational psychology. *Psychological Science in the Public Interest, 14*(1), 4–58.

Dweck, C. S. (2000). *Self theories: Their role in motivation, personality, and development.* New York: Taylor & Francis.

Ebbinghaus, H. (1964). *Memory: A contribution to experimental psychology.* New York: Dover. (Original work published 1885.)

Ekstrom, R. B., Goertz, M. E., Pollack, J. M., & Rock, D. A. (1986). Who drops out of high school and why? Findings of a national study. *Teachers College Record, 87*(3), 356–371.

Engel, S. (2011). Children's need to know: Curiosity in schools. *Harvard Educational Review, 81*(4), 625–645.

Engel, S. (2015). *The hungry mind.* Cambridge, MA: Harvard University Press.

Ericsson, K. A., Prietula, M. J., & Cokely, E. T. (2007). The making of an expert. *Harvard Business Review, 85*(7/8), 114–121.

Ericsson, K. A, Roring, R. W., & Nandagopal, K. (2007). Giftedness and evidence for reproducibly superior performance: An account based on the expert performance framework. *High Ability Studies, 18*(1), 3–56.

Faxon-Mills, S., Hamilton, L. S., Rudnick, M., & Stecher, B. M. (2013). *New assessments, better instruction? Designing assessment systems to promote instructional improvement.* Santa Monica, CA: RAND.

Finn, J. D., & Rock, D. A. (1997). Academic success among students at risk for school failure. *Journal of Applied Psychology, 82*(2), 221–234.

Fisher, D., & Frey, N. (2011). Checking for understanding. *Principal Leadership, 12*(1), 60–62.

Fredrickson, B. L., & Branigan, C. (2005). Positive emotions broaden the scope of attention and thought-action repertoires. *Cognition & Emotion, 19*(3), 313–332.

Frerejean, J., Brand-Gruwel, S., & Kirschner, P. A. (2013). *Fostering information problem-solving skills: Effects of worked examples and learner support.* Retrieved from http://dspace.ou.nl /bitstream/1820/5196/1/Summary-EARLI2013_JimmyFrerejean.pdf

Fuchs, L. S., Fuchs, D., Finelli, R., Courey, S. J., Hamlett, C. L., Sones, E. M., & Hope, S. (2006). Teaching 3rd graders about real-life mathematical problem solving: A randomized controlled study. *Elementary School Journal, 106*, 293–312.

Fritz, C. O., Morris, P. E., Nolan, D., & Singleton, J. (2007). Expanding retrieval practice: An effective aid to preschool children's learning. *Quarterly Journal of Experimental Psychology, 60*(7), 991–1004.

Fryer, R. G. (2013). Teacher incentives and student achievement: Evidence from New York City public schools. *Journal of Labor Economics, 31*(2), 373–407.

Fyfe, E. R., McNeil, N. M., Son, J. Y., & Goldstone, R. L. (2014). Concreteness fading in mathematics and science instruction: A systematic review. *Educational Psychology Review, 26*(1), 9–25.

Gates, A. I. (1917). Recitation as a factor in memorizing. *Archives of Psychology, 6* (40) 1–104.

Gentner, D., Loewenstein, J., & Thompson, L. (2003). Learning and transfer: A general role for analogical encoding. *Journal of Educational Psychology, 95*, 393–408.

Gentry, J. W., Burns, A. C., Dickinson, J. R., Putrevu, S., Chu, S., Hongyan, Y., et al. (2002). Managing the curiosity gap does matter: What do we need to do about it? *Developments in Business Simulation and Experiential Learning, 29*(1), 67–73.

Gilovich, T., Vallone, R., & Tversky, A. (1985). The hot hand in basketball: On the misperception of random sequences. *Cognitive Psychology, 17*(3), 295–314.

Gingerich, K. J., Bugg., J. M., Doe, S. R., Rowland, C. A., Richards, T. L., Tompkins, S. A., & McDaniel, M. A. (2014). Active processing via write-to-learn assignments: Learning and retention benefits in introductory psychology. *Teaching of Psychology, 41*(4), 303–308.

Godden, D. R., & Baddeley, A. D. (1975). Context-dependent memory in two natural environments: On land and underwater. *British Journal of Psychology, 66*, 325–331.

Goleman, D. (2013). *Focus: The hidden driver of excellence.* New York: Harper.

Goodwin, B., & Hubbell, E. R. (2013). *The 12 touchstones of good teaching: A checklist for staying focused every day*. Alexandria, VA: ASCD.

Gorman, A. M. (1961). Recognition memory for nouns as a function of abstractness and frequency. *Journal of Experimental Psychology, 61*, 23–29.

Graham, S., & Hebert, M. A. (2010). *Writing to read: Evidence for how writing can improve reading*. A Carnegie Corporation Time to Act Report. Washington, DC: Alliance for Excellent Education.

Greenberg, J., Pomerance, L., & Walsh, K. (2016). *Learning about learning: What every new teacher needs to know*. Washington, DC: National Council on Teacher Quality.

Haidt, J. (2006). *The happiness hypothesis: Finding modern truth in ancient wisdom*. New York: Basic Books.

Hamre, B. K., & Pianta, R. C. (2001). Early teacher–child relationships and the trajectory of children's school outcomes through eighth grade. *Child Development, 72*(2), 625–638.

Hamre, B. K., & Pianta, R. C. (2005). Can instructional and emotional support in the first-grade classroom make a difference for children at risk of school failure? *Child Development, 76*(5), 949–967.

Hartlep K. L., & Forsyth G. A. (2000). The effect of self-reference on learning and retention. *Teaching of Psychology, 27*, 269–271.

Harvard University Department of Psychology. (n.d.). George Miller. Retrieved from https://psychology.fas.harvard.edu/people/george-miller

Hattie, J. (2009). *Visible learning: A synthesis of over 800 meta-analyses relating to achievement*. New York: Routledge.

Hattie, J. (2012). *Visible learning for teachers: Maximizing impact on learning*. New York: Routledge.

Heller, N. (2017, August 9). Getting tanked: One writer's 60 minutes in sensory deprivation. *Vogue*. Retrieved from www.vogue.com/article/sensory-deprivation-tanks-float-spa

Hilbert, M., & Lopez, P. (2011). The world's technological capacity to store, communicate, and compute information. *Science, 332*(6025), 60–65.

Holyoak, K. J. (2005). Analogy. In K. J. Holyoak & R. G. Morrison (Eds.), *The Cambridge handbook of thinking and reasoning* (pp. 117–142). New York: Cambridge University Press.

Horne, B. (2019, January 2). Live blog of the fourth and final test between Australia v India. *The Daily Telegraph*. Retrieved from www.heraldsun.com.au/sport/cricket/live-blog-of-the-fourth-and-final-test-between-australia-v-india/live-coverage/a340ab75e5889b55db17f1f6e444304a

Hsu, Y.-S. (2008). Learning about seasons in a technologically enhanced environment: The impact of teacher-guided and student-centered instructional approaches on the process of students' conceptual change. *Science Education, 92*(2), 320–344.

Hyde, T. S., & Jenkins, J. J. (1969). Differential effects of incidental tasks on the organization of recall of a list of highly associated words. *Journal of Experimental Psychology, 82*, 472–481.

Isen, A. M., Daubman, K. A., & Nowicki, G. P. (1987). Positive affect facilitates creative problem solving. *Journal of Personality and Social Psychology, 52*, 1122–1131.

Isen, A. M., Shalker, T. E., Clark, M., & Karp, L. (1978). Affect, accessibility of material in memory, and behavior: A cognitive loop? *Journal of Personality and Social Psychology, 36*(1), 1.

James, K. H., & Engelhardt, L. (2012). The effects of handwriting experience on functional brain development in pre-literate children. *Trends in Neuroscience and Education, 1*(1), 32–42.

Jason, Z. (2017, Winter). Bored out of their minds. *Harvard Ed., 156*, 18–22, 24–26.

Johnson, D. W., Maruyama, G., Johnson, R., Nelson, D., & Skon, L. (1981). Effects of cooperative, competitive, and individualistic goal structures on achievement: A meta-analysis. *Psychological Bulletin, 89*(1), 47.

Jones, M. G. (1990). Action zone theory, target students and science classroom interactions. *Journal of Research in Science Teaching, 27*(8), 651–660.

Joyce, B., & Showers, B. (2002). *Student achievement through staff development* (3rd ed.). Alexandria, VA: ASCD.

Kahneman, D. (2011). *Thinking fast and slow.* New York: Farrar, Straus & Giroux.

Karpicke, J. D. (2012). Retrieval-based learning: Active retrieval promotes meaningful learning. *Current Directions in Psychological Science, 21,* 157–163.

Karpicke, J. D., Blunt, J. R., & Smith, M. A. (2016). Retrieval-based learning: positive effects of retrieval practice in elementary school children. *Frontiers in Psychology, 7,* 350.

Karpicke, J. D., Butler, A. C., & Roediger, H. L. (2009). Metacognitive strategies in student learning: Do students practice retrieval when they study on their own? *Memory, 17*(4), 471–479.

Kelly, S., & Turner, J. (2009). Rethinking the effects of classroom activity structure on the engagement of low-achieving students. *Teachers College Record, 111*(7), 1665–1692.

Kerr, R., & Booth, B. (1978). Specific and varied practice of a motor skill. *Perceptual and Motor Skills, 46*(2), 395–401.

King, A. (1991). Improving lecture comprehension: Effects of a meta-cognitive strategy. *Applied Cognitive Psychology, 5*(4), 331–346.

Kirschner, P. A., Sweller, J., & Clark, R. E. (2006). Why minimal guidance during instruction does not work: An analysis of the failure of constructivist, discovery, problem-based, experiential, and inquiry-based teaching. *Educational Psychologist, 41*(2), 75–86.

Klein, G. (1998). *Sources of power: How people make decisions.* Cambridge, MA: MIT Press.

Kleinfeld, J. (1972). *Instructional style and the intellectual performance of Indian and Eskimo students.* Washington, DC: U.S. Department of Health, Education, and Welfare, Office of Education, National Center for Educational Research and Development.

Klem, A. M., & Connell, J. P. (2004). Relationships matter: Linking teacher support to student engagement and achievement. *Journal of School Health, 74*(7), 262–273.

Kobayashi, K. (2006). Combined effects of note-taking/reviewing on learning and the enhancement through interventions: A meta-analytic review. *Educational Psychology, 26*(3), 459–477.

Kohn, A. (1999). *Punished by rewards: The trouble with gold stars, incentive plans, A's, praise, and other bribes.* Boston: Houghton Mifflin Harcourt.

Kounin, J. S. (1970). *Discipline and group management in classrooms.* New York: Holt, Rinehart & Winston.

Kruger, J., & Dunning, D. (1999). Unskilled and unaware of it: How difficulties in recognizing one's own incompetence lead to inflated self-assessments. *Journal of Personality and Social Psychology, 77*(6), 1121–1134.

Kulik, J. A., & Kulik, C. (1998). Timing of feedback and verbal learning. *Review of Educational Research, 58*(1), 79–97.

Langer, J. A., & Applebee, A. N. (1987). *How writing shapes thinking: A study of teaching and learning.* NCTE research report no. 22. Washington, DC: National Institute of Education.

Larwin, K. H., Dawson, D., Erickson, M., & Larwin, D. A. (2012). Impact of guided notes on achievement in K–12 and special education students. *International Journal of Special Education, 27*(3), 108–119.

Lemov, D. (2010). *Teach like a champion: 49 techniques that put students on the path to college.* San Francisco: Jossey-Bass.

Lesgold, A., Rubinson, J., Feltovich, P., et al. (1988). Expertise in a complex skill: Diagnosing X-ray pictures. In M. T. H. Chi, R. Glaser, & M. J. Farr (Eds.), *The nature of expertise* (pp. 311–342). Hillsdale, NJ: Erlbaum.

Leven, T., & Long, R. (1981). *Effective instruction.* Alexandria, VA: ASCD.

Levitin, D. J. (2015, September 23). Why it's so hard to pay attention, explained by science. *Fast Company.* Retrieved from www.fastcompany.com/3051417/why-its-so-hard-to-pay-attention-explained-by-science

Ling, L. M., Chik, P., & Pang, M. F. (2006). Patterns of variation in teaching the colour of light to Primary 3 students. *Instructional Science: An International Journal of Learning and Cognition, 34*(1), 1–19.

Locke, E. A., & Latham, G. P. (2006). New directions in goal-setting theory. *Current Directions in Psychological Science, 15*(5), 265–268.

Loewenstein, G. (1994). The psychology of curiosity: A review and reinterpretation. *Psychology Bulletin, 116*(1), 75–98.

Lowry, N., & Johnson, D. W. (1981). Effects of controversy on epistemic curiosity, achievement, and attitudes. *Journal of Social Psychology, 115,* 31–43.

Lubin, G. (2017, August 6). Blindfold chess king reveals his memory tricks. *Inverse.* Retrieved from www.inverse.com/article/29863-timur-gareyev-blindfold-chess-memory

Lyons, L. (2004, June 8). Most teens associate school with boredom, fatigue [blog post]. *Gallup Organization.* Retrieved from https://news.gallup.com/poll/11893/most-teens-associate-school-boredom-fatigue.aspx

Maheady, L., Mallette, B., Harper, G. F., & Sacca, K. (1991). Heads-together: A peer-mediated option for improving the academic achievement of heterogeneous learning groups. *Remedial and Special Education, 12*(2), 25–33.

Marin, L. M., & Halpern, D. F. (2011). Pedagogy for developing critical thinking in adolescents: Explicit instruction produces greatest gains. *Thinking Skills and Creativity, 6*(2011), 1–13.

Marx, R. W., Blumenfeld, P. C., Krajcik, J. S., Fishman, B., Soloway, E., Geier, R., et al. (2004). Inquiry-based science in the middle grades: Assessment of learning in urban systemic reform. *Journal of Research in Science Teaching, 41*(10), 1063–1080.

Marzano, R. J. (1998). *A theory-based meta-analysis of research on instruction.* Aurora, CO: Mid-continent Research for Education and Learning.

Marzano, R. J., Pickering, D. J., & Pollock, J. E. (2001). *Classroom instruction that works: Research-based strategies for increasing student achievement.* Alexandria, VA: ASCD.

Maslow, A. (1954). *Motivation and personality.* New York: Harper.

Mason, L. H., Snyder, K. H., Sukhram, D. P., & Kedem, Y. (2006). TWA + PLANS strategies for expository reading and writing: Effects for nine 4th-grade students. *Exceptional Children, 73*(1), 69–89.

Mastin, L. (n.d.). Memory encoding. Retrieved from www.human-memory.net/processes_encoding.html

Mayer, R. E. (2011). *Applying the science of learning.* Boston: Pearson/Allyn & Bacon.

Mbajiorgu, N. M., Ezechi, N. G., & Idoko, E. C. (2007). Addressing nonscientific presuppositions in genetics using a conceptual change strategy. *Science Education, 91*(3), 419–438.

McDaniel, M. A., Agarwal, P. K., Huelser, B. J., McDermott, K. B., & Roediger, H. L. (2011). Test-enhanced learning in a middle school science classroom: The effects of quiz frequency and placement. *Journal of Educational Psychology, 103,* 399–414.

McDaniel, M. A., & Donnelly, C. M. (1996). Learning with analogy and elaborative interrogation. *Journal of Educational Psychology, 88,* 508–519.

McDermott, K. B., Agarwal, P. K., D'Antonio, L., Roediger, H. L., & McDaniel, M. A. (2014). Both multiple-choice and short-answer quizzes enhance later exam performance in middle and high school classes. *Journal of Experimental Psychology: Applied, 20*(1), 3.

McGill, R. M. (2011). Pose, pause, pounce, bounce! [blog post]. *@TeacherToolkit*. Retrieved from www.teachertoolkit.co.uk/2011/11/04/pose-pause-bounce-pounce

McKee, R. (1997). *Story: Substance, structure, style and the principles of screenwriting.* New York: HarperCollins.

McRobbie, L. R. (2017, February 8). Total recall: The people who never forget. *The Guardian.* Retrieved from www.theguardian.com/science/2017/feb/08/total-recall-the-people-who -never-forget

McTighe, J., & Wiggins, G. (2013). *Essential questions: Opening doors to student understanding.* Alexandria, VA: ASCD.

Medina, J. (2008). *Brain rules: 12 principles for surviving and thriving at work, home, and school.* Seattle, WA: Pear Press.

Meyer, B. J. F., Middlemiss, W., Theodorou, E., Brezinski, K. L., McDougall, J., & Bartlett, B. J. (2002). Effects of structure strategy instruction delivered to 5th-grade children using the internet with and without the aid of older adult tutors. *Journal of Educational Psychology, 94*(3), 486–519.

Meyer, B. J. F., & Poon, L. W. (2001). Effects of structure strategy training and signaling on recall of text. *Journal of Educational Psychology, 93*, 141–159.

Miller, G. A. (1956). The magical number seven, plus or minus two: Some limits on our capacity for processing information. *Psychological Review, 63*(2), 81.

Miller, T. M., & Geraci, L. (2011, January 24). Unskilled but aware: Reinterpreting overconfidence in low-performing students. *Journal of Experimental Psychology: Learning, Memory, and Cognition, 37*(2), 502–506.

Miranda, A., Villaescusa, M., & Vidal-Abarca, E. (1997). Is attribution retraining necessary? Use of self-regulation procedures for enhancing the reading comprehension strategies of children with learning disabilities. *Journal of Learning Disabilities, 30*(5), 503–512.

Moreno, R., & Mayer, R. E. (2000). A coherence effect in multimedia learning: The case for minimizing irrelevant sounds in the design of multimedia instructional messages. *Journal of Educational Psychology, 92*(1), 117.

Mueller, P. A., & Oppenheimer, D. M. (2014 , May 22). The pen is mightier than the keyboard: Advantages of longhand over laptop note taking. *Psychological Science.*

National Institute of Child Health and Human Development. (2000). *Report of the National Reading Panel: Teaching children to read: An evidence-based assessment of the scientific research literature on reading and its implications for reading instruction.* Washington, DC: Author. Retrieved from www.nichd.nih.gov/publications/nrp/smallbook.htm

Nelson, T. O., & Leonesio, R. J. (1988). Allocation of self-paced study time and the "labor-in-vain effect." *Journal of Experimental Psychology, 14*(4), 676–686.

Newell, A., & Simon, H. A. (1972). *Human problem solving.* Englewood Cliffs, NJ: Prentice Hall.

Nokes, T. J., Schunn, C. D., & Chi, M. T. (2010). Problem solving and human expertise. *International Encyclopedia of Education* (Vol. 5, pp. 265–272). New York: Elsevier Science.

Paivio, A. (1971). *Imagery and verbal processes.* New York: Holt, Rinehart & Winston.

Parker, E. S., Cahill, L., & McGaugh, J. L. (2006). A case of unusual autobiographical remembering. *Neurocase, 12*(1), 35–49.

Pashler, H., Rohrer, D., Cepeda, N. J., & Carpenter, S. K. (2007). Enhancing learning and retarding forgetting: Choices and consequences. *Psychonomic Bulletin and Review, 14,* 187–193.

Patall, E., Cooper, H., & Robinson, J. C. (2008). The effects of choice on intrinsic motivation and related outcomes: A meta-analysis of research findings. *Psychological Bulletin, 134*(2), 270–300.

Pate, M. L., & Miller, G. (2011). Effects of regulatory self-questioning on secondary-level students' problem-solving performance. *Journal of Agricultural Education, 52*(1), 72–84.

Pearsall, G. (2018). *Fast and effective assessment*. Alexandria, VA: ASCD.

Pecheone, R., & Kahl, S. (2014). Where are we now: Lessons learned and emerging directions. In L. Darling-Hammond & F. Adamson (Eds.), *Beyond the bubble test: How performance assessments support 21st century learning* (pp. 53–91). San Francisco: Jossey-Bass.

Pellegrino, A. M. (2007). *The manifestation of critical thinking and metacognition in secondary American history students through the implementation of lesson plans and activities consistent with historical thinking skills*. Unpublished doctoral dissertation, Florida State University.

Piaget, J. (1972). Intellectual evolution from adolescence to adulthood. *Human Development, 15*(1), 1–12.

Pine, J. (2015, November 16–29). My mistake. *Nursery World,* 21–24.

Pink, D. H. (2011). *Drive: The surprising truth about what motivates us.* New York: Riverhead Books.

Pressley, M., McDaniel, M. A., Turnure, J. E., Wood, E., & Ahmad, M. (1987). Generation and precision of elaboration: Effects on intentional and incidental learning. *Journal of Experimental Psychology: Learning, Memory, and Cognition, 13,* 291–300.

Queensland Brain Institute. (n.d.). How are memories formed? Retrieved from https://qbi.uq.edu.au/brain-basics/memory/how-are-memories-formed

Quitadamo, I. J., & Kurtz, M. J. (2007). Learning to improve: Using writing to increase critical thinking performance in general education biology. *CBE—Life Sciences Education, 6*(2), 140–154.

Reber, P. (2010, May 1). What is the memory capacity of the human brain? *Scientific American.* Retrieved from www.scientificamerican.com/article/what-is-the-memory-capacity

Renkl, A. (2005). The worked-out examples principle in multimedia learning. In R. E. Mayer (Ed.), *The Cambridge handbook of multimedia learning.* Cambridge: Cambridge University Press.

Renkl, A., Atkinson, R. K., & Große, C. S. (2004). How fading worked solution steps works: A cognitive load perspective. *Instructional Science, 32*(1–2), 59–82.

Richards, B. A., & Frankland, P. W. (2017). The persistence and transience of memory. *Neuron, 94*(6), 1071–1084.

Richardson, M., Abraham, C., & Bond, R. (2012). Psychological correlates of university students' academic performance: A systematic review and meta-analysis. *Psychological Bulletin, 138*(2), 353–387.

Rivet, A. E., & Krajcik, J. S. (2004). Achieving standards in urban systemic reform: An example of a 6th grade project-based science curriculum. *Journal of Research in Science Teaching, 41*(7), 669–692.

Roediger, H. L., & Pyc, M. A. (2012). Inexpensive techniques to improve education: Applying cognitive psychology to enhance educational practice. *Journal of Applied Research in Memory and Cognition, 1*(4), 242–248.

Rogers, T. B., Kuiper, N. A., & Kirker, W. S. (1977). Self-reference and the encoding of personal information. *Journal of Personality and Social Psychology, 35,* 677–688.

Rohrer, D., & Pashler, H. (2010). Recent research on human learning challenges conventional instructional strategies. *Educational Researcher, 39*(5), 406–412.

Rosenshine, B., Meister, C., & Chapman, S. (1996). Teaching students to generate questions: A review of the intervention studies. *Review of Educational Research, 66,* 181–221.

Rowe, M. B. (1986). Wait time: slowing down may be a way of speeding up! *Journal of Teacher Education, 37*(1), 43–50.

Rule, A. C., & Furletti, C. (2004). Using form and function analogy object boxes to teach human body systems. *School Science and Mathematics, 104*(4), 155–169.

Sample, I. (2016, November 16). Inside the brain of the man who would be "Blindfold King" of chess. *The Guardian*. Retrieved from www.theguardian.com/science/2016/nov/03/inside-the-brain-of-the-man-who-would-be-blindfold-king-of-chess-timur-gareyev

Schmoker, M. (2011). *Focus: Elevating the essentials to radically improve student learning*. Alexandria, VA: ASCD.

Schroeder, C. M., Scott, T. P., Tolson, H., Huang, T.-Y., & Lee, Y.-H. (2007). A meta-analysis of national research: Effects of teaching strategies on student achievement in science in the United States. *Journal of Research in Science Teaching, 44*(10), 1436–1460.

Schwartz, N., Stroud, M., Hong, N., Lee, T., Scott, B., & McGee, S. (2006). Summoning prior knowledge: The influence of metaphorical priming on learning in a hypermedia environment. *Journal of Educational Computing Research, 35*(1), 1–30.

Schworm, S., & Renkl, A. (2006). Computer-supported example-based learning: When instructional explanations reduce self-explanations. *Computers & Education, 46*(4), 426–445.

Scruggs, T. E., Mastropieri, M. A., & Sullivan, G. S. (1994). Promoting relational thinking: Elaborative interrogation for students with mild disabilities. *Exceptional Children, 60*, 450–457.

Seligman, M. E. (1990). *Learned optimism: The skills to conquer life's obstacles, large and small*. New York: Random House.

Sencibaugh, J. M. (2007). Meta-analysis of reading comprehension for students with learning disabilities: Strategies and implications. *Reading Improvement, 44*(1), 6–22.

Shute, V. J. (2008). Focus on formative feedback. *Review of Educational Research, 78*(1), 153–189.

Silver, E. A. (1979). Student perceptions of relatedness among verbal problems. *Journal of Research in Mathematics Education, 10*, 195–210.

Silver, H. F., Abla, C., Boutz, A. L., & Perini, M. J. (2018). *Tools for classroom instruction that works*. Franklin Lakes, NJ: Thoughtful Education Press.

Smith, L. K. C., & Fowler, S. A. (1984). Positive peer pressure: The effects of peer monitoring on children's disruptive behavior. *Journal of Applied Behavior Analysis, 17*(2), 213–227.

Smith, B. L., Holliday, W. G., & Austin, H. W. (2010). Students' comprehension of science textbooks using a question-based reading strategy. *Journal of Research in Science Teaching, 47*, 363–379.

Smith, S. M. (1982). Enhancement of recall using multiple environmental contexts during learning. *Memory & Cognition, 10*, 405–412.

Sousa, D. A. (2011). *How the brain learns* (4th ed.). Thousand Oaks, CA: Corwin.

Stevens, R. J., Slavin, R. E., & Farnish, A. M. (1991). The effects of cooperative learning and direct instruction in reading comprehension strategies on main idea identification. *Journal of Educational Psychology, 83*(1), 8.

Streeck-Fischer, A., & van der Kolk, B. A. (2000). Down will come baby, cradle and all: Diagnostic and therapeutic implications of chronic trauma on child development. *Australian and New Zealand Journal of Psychiatry, 34*(6), 903–918.

Suchan, B. (2018, November 15). Why don't we forget how to ride a bike? *Scientific American*. Retrieved from www.scientificamerican.com/article/why-dont-we-forget-how-to-ride-a-bike

Sweller, J. (1988). Cognitive load during problem solving: Effects on learning. *Cognitive Science, 12*, 257–285.

Sweller, J., & Cooper, G. A. (1985). The use of worked examples as a substitute for problem solving in learning algebra. *Cognition and Instruction, 2*, 59–89.

Symons, C. S., & Johnson, B. T. (1997). The self-reference effect in memory: A meta-analysis. *Psychological Bulletin, 121*(3), 371–394.

Tarhan, L., & Acar, B. (2007). Problem-based learning in an 11th grade chemistry class: "Factors affecting cell potential." *Research in Science and Technology Education, 25*(3), 351–369.

Tarhan, L., Ayar-Kayali, H., Urek, R. O., & Acar, B. (2008). Problem-based learning in a 9th grade chemistry class: "Intermolecular forces." *Research in Science Education, 38*(3), 285–300.

Taylor, K., & Rohrer, D. (2010). The effects of interleaved practice. *Applied Cognitive Psychology, 24,* 837–848.

Twenge, J. M., Zhang, L., & Im, C. (2004). It's beyond my control: A cross-temporal meta-analysis of increasing externality in locus of control, 1960–2002. *Personality and Social Psychology Review, 8*(3) 308–319.

Um, E. R., Plass, J. L., Hayward, E. O., & Homer, B. D. (2012). Emotional design in multimedia learning. *Journal of Educational Psychology, 104*(2), 485–498.

University of New South Wales. (2012, November 28). Four is the "magic" number. *ScienceDaily.* Retrieved June 20, 2019, from www.sciencedaily.com/releases/2012/11/121128093930.htm

Urquhart, V., & Frazee, D. (2012). *Teaching reading in the content areas: If not me, then who?* (3rd ed.). Alexandria, VA: ASCD.

van Merrienboer, J. J. G., & Sweller, J. (2005). Cognitive load theory and complex learning: Recent developments and future directions. *Educational Psychology Review, 17*(2), 147–177.

Walsh, J. A., & Sattes, B. D. (2005). *Quality questioning: Research-based practices to engage every learner.* Thousand Oaks, CA: Corwin.

Wammes, J. D., Meade, M. E., & Fernandes, M. A. (2016). The drawing effect: Evidence for reliable and robust memory benefits in free recall. *Quarterly Journal of Experimental Psychology, 69*(9), 1752.

Wanzek, J., Wexler, J., Vaughn, S., & Ciullo, S. (2010). Reading interventions for struggling readers in the upper elementary grades: A synthesis of 20 years of research. *Reading and Writing, 23*(8), 889–812.

Ward, J. D., & Lee, C. L. (2004). Teaching strategies for FCS: Student achievement in problem-based learning versus lecture-based instruction. *Journal of Family and Consumer Sciences, 96*(1), 73–76.

Weinstein, Y., Gilmore, A. W., Szpunar, K. K., & McDermott, K. B. (2014). The role of test expectancy in the build-up of proactive interference in long-term memory. *Journal of Experimental Psychology: Learning, Memory, and Cognition, 40*(4), 1039–1048.

Weinstein, Y., Madan, C. R., & Sumeracki, M. A. (2018). Teaching the science of learning. *Cognitive Research: Principles and Implications, 3*(2), 1–17.

Wiliam, D. (2007). Content then process: Teacher learning communities in the service of formative assessment. In D. B. Reeves (Ed.), *Ahead of the curve: The power of assessment to transform teaching and learning* (pp. 183–204). Bloomington, IN: Solution Tree.

Willingham, D. (2003). Students remember . . . what they think about. *American Educator, 27*(2), 37–41.

Willingham, D. (2007). Critical thinking: Why is it so hard to teach? *American Educator,* 8–19.

Woloshyn, V., Paivio, A., & Pressley, M. (1994). Use of elaborative interrogation to help students acquire information consistent with prior knowledge and information inconsistent with prior knowledge. *Journal of Educational Psychology, 86*(1), 79–89.

Woloshyn, V. E., Pressley, M., & Schneider, W. (1992). Elaborative-interrogation and prior-knowledge effects on learning of facts. *Journal of Educational Psychology, 84*(1), 115–124.

Wong, R. M. F., Lawson, M. J., & Keeves, J. (2002). The effects of self-explanation training on students' problem solving in high-school mathematics. *Learning and Instruction, 12,* 233–262.

Wood, E., & Hewitt, K. L. (1993). Assessing the impact of elaborative strategy instruction relative to spontaneous strategy use in high achievers. *Exceptionality, 4*, 65–79.

Young, C. (2015, December 1). Don't forget, the science of memory is key to helping students learn. *The Guardian*. Retrieved from www.theguardian.com/teacher-network/2015/dec/01/dont -forget-science-memory-key-students-learn

Zhu, X., & Simon, H. A. (1987). Learning mathematics from examples and by doing. *Cognition and Instruction, 4*, 137–166.

Zimmer, C. (2017, February 2). The purpose of sleep? To forget, scientists say. *New York Times*, p. D5. Retrieved from www.nytimes.com/2017/02/02/science/sleep-memory-brain-forgetting.html

Index

The letter *f* following a page locator denotes a figure. Toolkit strategies are entered in all caps.

About the Authors

 **Bryan Goodwin** is the president and CEO of McREL International, a Denver-based nonprofit education research and development organization. Goodwin, a former teacher and journalist, has been at McREL for more than 20 years, serving previously as chief operating officer and director of communications and marketing.

He has authored or coauthored several books, including *Unstuck: How Curiosity, Peer Coaching and Teaming Can Change Your School, Simply Better: Doing What Matters Most to Change the Odds for Student Success, The 12 Touchstones of Good Teaching: A Checklist for Staying Focused Every Day, Balanced Leadership for Powerful Learning: Tools for Achieving Success in Your School,* and *The Future of Schooling: Educating America in 2020.* Goodwin writes a monthly research column for *Educational Leadership* and presents research findings and insights to audiences across the United States and in Canada, the Middle East, and Australia.

 **Tonia Gibson** served as a teacher and assistant principal at primary schools in Melbourne, Australia. As a member of McREL International's learning services team, she supports education ministries, district leaders, school leaders, and teachers across the U.S. and Micronesia in using research to improve professional practices and support systemic improvement. In addition to leading workshops and presenting at conferences, she has developed practical guides and materials for teachers and leaders and coauthored *Unstuck: How Curiosity, Peer Coaching, and Teaming Can Change Your School.*

 **Kristin Rouleau** serves as the executive director of learning services and innovation at McREL International, where she guides a team of consultants who help schools, districts, and state education agencies and ministries of education across the United States, Canada, Micronesia, Australia, the Middle East, and China translate research into solutions that transform teaching, leading, and learning. A licensed school administrator with more than 25 years of classroom and school leadership experience, she coauthored *Curiosity Works: A Guidebook for Moving Your School from Improvement to Innovation* and *Unstuck: How Curiosity, Peer Coaching, and Teaming Can Change Your School.*

About McREL

McREL International is an internationally recognized, nonprofit education research and development organization, headquartered in Denver, Colorado, with offices in Honolulu, Hawai'i and Cheyenne, Wyoming. Since 1966, McREL has helped translate research and professional wisdom about what works in education into practical guidance for educators. Our expert staff members and affiliates include respected researchers, experienced consultants, and published writers who provide educators with research-based guidance, consultation, and professional development for improving student outcomes.

Related ASCD Resources: Brain-Based Instructional Design

At the time of publication, the following resources were available (ASCD stock numbers in parentheses). For up-to-date information about ASCD resources, go to www.ascd.org. You can search the complete archives of *Educational Leadership* at www.ascd.org/el.

Print Products

The 12 Touchstones of Good Teaching: A Checklist for Staying Focused Every Day by Bryan Goodwin and Elizabeth Ross Hubbell (#113009)

Attack of the Teenage Brain!: Understanding and Supporting the Weird and Wonderful Adolescent Learner by John Medina (#118024)

Balanced Leadership for Powerful Learning: Tools for Achieving Success in Your School by Bryan Goodwin and Greg Cameron with Heather Hein (#112025)

Classroom Instruction That Works, 2nd Edition by Ceri B. Dean, Elizabeth Ross Hubbell, Howard Pitler, and Bj Stone (#111001)

Differentiation and the Brain: How Neuroscience Supports the Learner-Friendly Classroom, 2nd Edition by David A. Sousa and Carol Ann Tomlinson (#318125)

Engage the Brain: How to Design for Learning That Taps into the Power of Emotion by Allison Posey (#119015)

A Handbook for Classroom Instruction That Works by Howard Pitler and Bj Stone (#112013)

The Motivated Brain: Improving Student Attention, Engagement, and Perseverance by Gayle Gregory and Martha Kaufeldt (#115041)

Simply Better: Doing What Matters Most to Change the Odds for Student Success by Bryan Goodwin (#111038)

Unstuck: How Curiosity, Peer Coaching, and Teaming Can Change Your School by Bryan Goodwin, Kristin Rouleau, Dale Lewis, and Tonia Gibson (#118036)

Using Brain Science to Make Learning Stick (Quick Reference Guide) by Bryan Goodwin and Tonia Gibson (#QRG120087)

ASCD myTeachSource®

Download resources from a professional learning platform with hundreds of research-based best practices and tools for your classroom at http://myteachsource.ascd.org/.

For more information, send an e-mail to member@ascd.org; call 1-800-933-2723 or 703-578-9600; send a fax to 703-575-5400; or write to Information Services, ASCD, 1703 N. Beauregard St., Alexandria, VA 22311-1714 USA.

THE WHOLE CHILD

The ASCD Whole Child approach is an effort to transition from a focus on narrowly defined academic achievement to one that promotes the long-term development and success of all children. Through this approach, ASCD supports educators, families, community members, and policymakers as they move from a vision about educating the whole child to sustainable, collaborative actions.

Learning That Sticks relates to the **supported** and **challenged** tenets. *For more about the ASCD Whole Child approach, visit* **www.ascd.org/wholechild.**

WHOLE CHILD
TENETS

1 HEALTHY
Each student enters school healthy and learns about and practices a healthy lifestyle.

2 SAFE
Each student learns in an environment that is physically and emotionally safe for students and adults.

3 ENGAGED
Each student is actively engaged in learning and is connected to the school and broader community.

4 SUPPORTED
Each student has access to personalized learning and is supported by qualified, caring adults.

5 CHALLENGED
Each student is challenged academically and prepared for success in college or further study and for employment and participation in a global environment.

LEARN. TEACH. LEAD.